Christian Hauvette

dwellings−monuments−machines | truth−metaphor−narrative

Preface by
Alice Laguarda and Paul Ardenne

Texts by
Denis Pondruel
Didier Laroque
Stan Neumann
Christian Hauvette

Photographs by
Nicolas Borel
Georges Fessy
Marcus Robinson

Birkhäuser−Publishers for Architecture
Basel · Boston · Berlin

dwellings

monuments

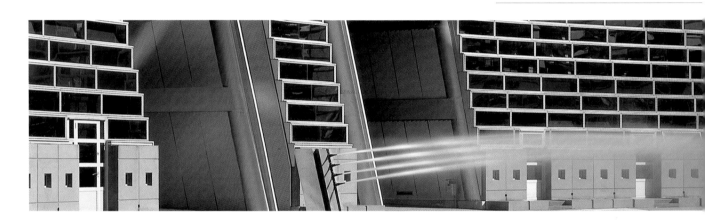

machines

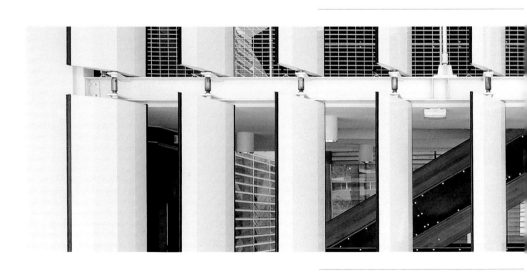

Catalogue | Decalogue

The Architecture of Hauvette: Ten Stations as Code

Alice Laguarda and Paul Ardenne

Education Authority
of Martinique,
Fort-de-France
(wind box)

1 | Primitive figure

If one considers architecture as an expression of a primitive and universal figure, such as box, trunk, container or as the "principle of all things" (architecture coming from *arkhé*, principle, beginning), then architecture would serve essentially to cover, to encompass, to contain, to protect *being*. It would be the act that signifies and marks the limit between an inside and an outside, between an interior and an exterior. Serving alternatively as metaphor for the first container, for the maternal womb, for the earthly cradle, for the sarcophagus that joins the worlds of the living and the dead, architecture would preserve the secret of an intimacy (drawing its sense here from a second etymological root, *arceo*: I contain, and *arcanum:* the secret).

One might imagine that architecture consists in a series of infinite variations on this theme of the original box. But equating architecture with such a variation on a single symbol would presuppose that geometry's only value lies in line; this would imply that the variations of a work can only take place inside a frame, an ideal enclosure. Only in relation to the ideal model of the box would a work exist; of this model the work would be merely a pale reflection, a feeble approach, and its only value would lie in its relation to this model which it seeks to attain.

The function of geometry in the work of Christian Hauvette is, above all, poetic: the architecture addresses itself to the *flâneur*, to the strolling passer-by. The "wind box" building (Education Authority of Martinique, Fort-de-France, 1989-94) is organized around a series of variations on a system of slatted blinds– typical of Martinique– but which, above all, by their half-open form, qualify the spaces. In this instance, architecture ceases to be an isolated act marking the sharp separation of a "refuge" from the outside world. Undoubtedly, one must break with the fossilized monumental structure that results from a reductive interpretation of the original form. The plan and volume of the wind box, its intervals and sections, alive with curving bends and openings –the box is pierced, perforated, open to the atmosphere, crisscrossed by light and sound– create a space that encourages moments of psychological and physical liberty. It's as if the black box of the tomb … "*on the side of religious practices and civil laws regarding death,*" had transformed itself,

little by little, into a white box … "*on the side of the physis (Gr., phil. 'the natural form of a thing') in the light of the sun.*"[1] Can one say, for all that, that the secret no longer exists? That the mystery of the figure can be unveiled?

These are the known dangers of transparency in architecture: a pre-judged geometric form, possessing neither shadows nor secrets, equally transparent to sight and thought. Hiding nothing that exceeds the definition given in an easy formula, as if the work were merely a factual given, offering itself spontaneously to the glance of an observer– merely to be perceived, described, and assimilated. This is an illusion.

Thus the office building of the Savings and Loans Bank in Paris (1998-completion 2000), stretched in a long glass facade along the elevation that faces the Seine, is based on a subversion of the model (or almost, of the cliché) of the internal street. Here it is transformed into a broad and luminous slit which leads a double existence: diurnal (in the architect's creation) and nocturnal (in artist James Turrell's execution). Here the pure and abstract forms – "*models of simple ideas*"– are no longer "*known, seen, and understood without a residue,*" without matter and depth: "*the supposed realism of pure ideas becomes heavy and reassumes the density which the Platonic sun had dissolved.*"[2] From the white box, little by little, one returns towards the black box. The architectural object is not there to illuminate the context. The figure is not there to be redundant of the program, the use. Christian Hauvette exploits the reference to an original form in order to better dissect its normative illusions. "*My idea is rather to dramatize the way I struggle with the box (to make it deliver itself of its potential) to show through which specific assaults I invest in it. To let people guess at which ruses I use to circumvent it. To reveal the mask by which I deceive it.*"[3] The context thus made opaque, we find ourselves confronted by the very thing that escapes us, trapped in a continuous oscillation between an illusion of transparency and an illusion of opacity.

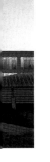

CEMAGREF-ENGREF
(Lafayette Polytechnic
School),
Clermont-Ferrand
(deliberative machine)

2 | Evaluation

How to evaluate Hauvette's architecture? To do so, one must explore the imprint left by the reference systems inevitably shared by any architect born into a 1940s heritage. In other words: 1) a consideration of the link between architecture and catastrophe, and of war as anti-architecture (Mars, that great anti-architect); 2) the wakening of his conscience in a western world that needed to be reconstructed and which was dedicated to the great projects of the *Trente Glorieuses* – the thirty glorious postwar years of economic growth – where cities, that had been destroyed only yesterday, became the many laboratories for experimental architecture (the breeding-grounds of Le Havre, Frankfurt, Essen, Dunkirk, Hiroshima); 3) his studies undertaken in universities in theoretical conflict: on the one hand, the professor-architects who had never recovered from Loos' anti-ornamentalism (a "crime," as we all know), and, on the other hand, the acolytes of triumphant functionalism (the Bauhaus ideology, the International Modern or International Style and its tutelary divinities such as Gropius, Le Corbusier, Niemeyer); 4) the shock of post-modernism, sweeping through the late 1970s like a liberating breeze, by Rossi, Mendini, and others – Charles Moore: a horrible rebirth of pointless citation, greco-roman pillars, Wren-like pediments – but an invitation, in any case, to throw everything overboard, immediately: the baby ("modern" architecture) and the bath water (the dictatorship of "modernism").

All of Hauvette's architecture echoes with these complex references calibrating both necessity and opportunity, offering both the mood of ending modernity and an opening towards a grammar of construction henceforth qualified by rules that are in tension, and more contradictory than homogeneous. This is architecture that one can qualify as "deliberative," exploiting those principles which have become fashionable in all contemporary creation: the absence of an imperative or pre-defined stylistic program, priority given to the process of creation, the building conceived as an object in dialogue with the surroundings, and apt to affirm itself in a single movement, thus working against or with the context. Specific examples? Conceived in function of its site on the heights of Schoelcher and because of its exposure to the trade wind, the Education Authority of Martinique in Fort-de-France (1989-94) displays a curve which is as monumental as it is functional, a form designed to automatically set the air in motion just as a propeller or the edge of an airplane wing would. The Lafayette Polytechnic School in Clermont-Ferrand (1988-91) creates a relationship between geometric forms in reference both to the most ancient traditions of organization (divide the spaces while maintaining their complementary nature) and to the imaginary universe of eternal architecture (the imprint of the eternal city is clear: one feels one is seeing the coliseum or the circus maximus). The whole presents itself as in debt to the cutting edge of technological investment, and to the most innovative techniques in mathematical calculation, equipment, and conception of materials. Nearby on the Céseaux Campus, one elevation of the School of Agricultural Engineering and Water and Forest Management (1994-98) alternates glass facades which resemble tobacco dryers in southern France with real trees set into the thickness of a wall where the mineral world cedes its place to the vegetable world… There is a tension towards improvisation within the limits, it goes without saying, of functionality and of the technical and administrative norms imposed on architecture in use. Tension also towards a synthesis, continually questioned, where ideology gives way to contextual practice. In this case, architecture is certainly "creation" in the modern sense (Paul Klee and the path towards form). Challenge, whimsy, token, everything merges and creates linkages. Hence, with regard to evaluating the work as a whole, no formula exists that might condense its totality into a stainless, cube-like – much less conclusive definition. Rather, Hauvette's architecture can be considered as a theoretic accumulator, a sculptural modulator. It is thought of as mobility: music, interpreted according to the art of the fugue.

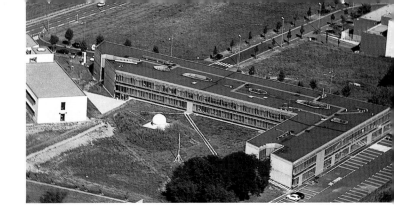

ENSIM
(National College of
Engeneering), Le Mans
(the "sign zero"
of architecture)

3 | Signature

The major fault – or curse, or perversity – of architecture is the signature. Certainly, any building can be perceived as a "sign" in public space, the sign of a presence, of a function, of a representation of power or of its opposite. Equally, it can be perceived as the creation of an individual, literally, as a signature. The first challenge of this inevitably individual dimension of architecture is certainly the name. This abuse – the imperative need for *distinction* – and here we use the term drawn from Pierre Bourdieu, one of his preferred criteria – has, at least since the renaissance, become a focal point.

Let us ask the question brutally: does Hauvette's architecture belong to this fatal tradition of *distinction*? Is his a method that aims, more than anything else, at fame? A Brunelleschi, a Borromini, or a Mies are recognizable even at a distance. So be it. This assertive process, this quest for recognition, this hubris of a proclaimed identity might, for all one knows, work against the glory of the builder: avowal of the heroic posture of the architect, of his demiurgic penchants, of the pride which works upon and which surreptitiously corrects the project. For its part, Hauvette's architecture seems to have happily buried such narcissistic tendencies. Its rejection of excess is innate: the form may be monumental (the 250-m-length of the French Development Agency near the Gare de Lyon in Paris), but it moderates any temptation towards gigantism by a subtle use of rhythm, scansion or repetition. Hauvette's mistrust of all spectacular inscriptions is equally clear. Is the epoch propitious for showy virtuosity and exacerbated signatures? François Lamarre on the ENSIM building (*L'École nationale supérieure des ingénieurs du Mans*, 1997): "*The ENSIM is a lesson in discretion and efficacy. Christian Hauvette wanted a 'non-existent' building in Italo Calvino's meaning of the word. In common with the author of 'The Nonexistent Knight' and 'Invisible Cities,' the architect has a mischievous tone and an economical style. On a campus where buildings have been vying to outdo each other for the last thirty years, he chose to abandon this competition of forms and to build a 'sign zero' building, an absence as it were in its environment.*"[4] The result is a simple building set at a right angle, unexpected in its context, though anticipated in its form, without any striking characteristics, except for the paradox-ical emptying of the principle of effect, here turned inside out like a glove, making this very paradox the building's strength.

The signature – let us interpret it as the pre-requisite not of an identity but of an existence dependent on the media. To be primed up, this type of existence requires the double tyranny of the "incomparable" and the "truly different." Where Hauvette's architecture challenges the apologetic of the "signature," it's not because it wishes to be radically different, but because it wishes to differentiate itself from all showy spectacle. Most often discreet, the approach belongs to the great modernist tradition: the forms are geometric; the materials – metal, glass, cement – are unmistakably contemporary; an unmasked primacy of high-tech over low-tech. These are all *a priori* characteristics of architectural poetics created not by difference but qualified, on the contrary, by encoding, by adherence to its time. A genetic agreement of architecture with the materials and the image of its period. This inflection might make one think of it as an architecture without qualities, a prudent, derivative, fashionable, and conformist product – a non-architecture. This would be quite the wrong impression. Above all, Hauvette's architecture defines itself as contemporaneous with Lyotard's end of the age of large-scale narratives. Hauvette's architecture prefers the infra-sign to the slogan, background noise to a street jamboree. The metaphor is clear: that of a collapse of the immemorial faith which made architecture into: the *magnum opus*. There is no purpose in adding grandiloquence to that which, in any case, nobody believes anymore. Rather than dissemble, it is better to merge with the thousand layers of contemporary culture. Sometimes it goes so far as to be nearly anonymous in a formulation where the tyranny of the "me/I" no longer has any purchase.

Faculty of Law
and Economics, Brest
(virtue of geometry)

4 | Polyhedrons

To sum up, Hauvette's architecture is more an initial than a signature. It indicates an identity without becoming emblematic or, for a stronger reason, an encumbrance: the public housing on the boulevard de Rennes (1992-96), for instance, so ordinary at first glance, reveals its complexity as soon as one has understood how the interior spaces are distributed as an inspired extension of Le Corbusier's theories on the domestic module as a "machine for living." This stanza, at times disabused, is an exercise carried out in the troubling light of a western civilization that is as conceptually unproductive as it is materially enterprising. The lesson of Christian Hauvette invariably reveals itself as marked by the imprint of high culture; this is the culture not of primitive Adam but of modern man, the most recent arrival, he who has seen everything, judged everything, meditated on everything. Western man, even in his most recent incarnation, is defined by his passage through heritage, by the enormous mental machinery of that which is already given, by the complex of a proliferating culture. A heritage merely to be smashed, they say … in jest, but surely. By all accounts the moderns have been no less conservative than the ancients were. This is clear from their taste for the archaic, for the primitive; from their respect for certain criteria, such as authenticity, precision, purity, and the ideal; from their devotional propensities; from their reverence for utopia; and from their desire to organize a universe beyond the merely human, creating, as if by a perfect bit of coincidence, something uncannily similar to the ideas of paradise perfected in the past by systems of the sacred, now supposedly obsolete.

A passage through heritage? For architecture, one might just as well say a necessary confrontation with certain questions like those regarding pure geometry, rigorous organization and polyhedrons, the unavoidable grammar of universal archi-tecture. As a consequence, a confrontation with the basic forms is inevitable on the practical level – the monolith, the faceted volume, and the clearly defined module – this is an evident Euclidean metaphor for eternity, for a world *ordered*, once and for all. The mental pressure, in this respect, is at its zenith. And, in this context, esthetics is joined by politics. Power, as we all know, loves these Platonic polyhedrons: the cube, the sphere, the pyramid, and the parallelepiped. "*These geometric or monolithic blocks*," Chantal Béret quite rightly reminds us, "*denote a desire to stand out, and to forget the conventions which traditionally create the texture of a city and insert a public building into its context. The ideological motive which aims at promoting these formal archetypes recalls the 'exemplum virtutis' vaunted by the rev-olutionary ideal in order to regenerate the arts though the original truth and elementary rationalism of neoclassicism in contrast to the decadence of the baroque canon. Platonic polyhedrons are beautiful because they are clear, perfect, eternal, precisely the opposite of historic, contingent forms.*"[5]

Looked at in relation to the polyhedrons, Hauvette's architecture always puts one off the scent. Here, the empire of geometry remains intact. It is totally different from the deconstructionism of a Gehry, for example. Nor is it the object of boundless admiration. Incomparably, the forms penetrate one another, feed off each other – the ravenous curve devouring the straight line – as in the facade of the Faculty of Law and Economics in Brest (1984-87). In other instances, the geometric form remains a mere suggestion: ends are absent, deviating forms multiply – one need only look at the curved walls of the nursery on the rue Saint-Maur (1986-90) which contrast with the loopholes arranged at right angles displayed on the facade of the building. Or, the tilt of the circular space of the Lafayette Polytechnic School of Clermont-Ferrand. Or, the surprising and unnatural overhang which tyrannizes the order of the rear facade of the Police Administrative building (Paris, 1991-94). Occasionally, a corner will take the liberty of overturning the discreet sculptural logic of a linear structure, as if the geometry were locked in a silent but stubborn confrontation with itself. Such is the case in the north facade of the Regional Chamber of Finance in Rennes (1985-88), a dynamic tableau reminiscent of El Lissitsky's famous poster "*Enfonce les Blancs avec un coin rouge.*" … It is a war between rules and caprice, as Francis Haskell would say, but it is guerrilla war, a war game at the limit of discretion, whose outcome is neither quest for power nor dynastic reform. The battle, never brutal, goes well beyond the ordinary logic of combat – victory. It plays tricks, it reactivates tensions, it rises, spectre-like, as the austere polyhedral dictum handed down through the ages (and demonstrates that one is not a dupe).

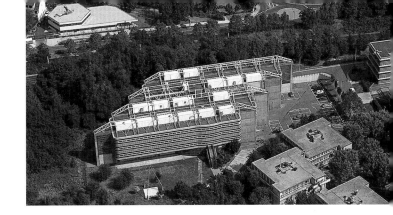

National College
Louis Lumière,
Noisy-le-Grand
(articulation,
composition)

5 | Double articulation

In his essay "*Complexity and Contradiction in Architecture*," Robert Venturi criticizes the ideological impasse of modern architecture, praising instead the virtues of complexity and ambivalence. He declares, "*to 'this or that' I prefer 'this and that,' to white or black I prefer white and black and sometimes gray. When architecture is successful, it elicits several levels of meaning and several varying and combined interpretations; one can read it and use its space and its elements in several different ways simultaneously.*"[6]

Many architects make use of this phenomenon of "simultaneity." But one must verify whether it is merely a way of lending legitimacy to an excessively efficient and mechanical esthetic.

When Christian Hauvette says he hopes that his architecture will manifest itself in a series of "relevant paradigms," he doubtlessly shares this same critical attitude towards the reductive academic tradition. These paradigms serve to represent the program in all its implications and hence in all its complexity: geometry, symbols, economy, construction, climate… Each project is thus organized in a system of articulations between a meaningful unity (the box or container – a key figure in modernity) and a series of distinct elements deprived of sense (walls, floors, pillars, roofs, staircases):

– In the National College Louis Lumière in Noisy-le-Grand (1986-88): the container is a diamond-shape lozenge and its structure is doubled (a Scottish plaid); a first envelope, a thin and transparent curtain in glass and aluminum echoes a metallic steel structure from which is suspended a metal roof.

– In the Faculty of Law and Economics in Brest (1984-87): the container consists of a series of eccentric curves, the center of each being planted on the arc of another; a sparsely perforated facade of smooth concrete echoes the structural framework, composed of white concrete columns and beams.

– In the Lafayette Polytechnic School in Clermont-Ferrand (1988-91): an ellipse is attached to a bar: the interior curve is covered with windows of reflecting glass, while the exterior wall is cladded with polished black concrete panels.

Architecture consists in experimenting with a series of articulations, whose confrontation will generate a story: a combinatory in which one enumerates, one connects, one divides elements into signifying units and distinctive units. Simple geometric figures are truncated, patterned, echoed. Frameworks can be massive or light, regular or irregular. Materials can be smooth or porous, unfinished or varnished, matte or shiny. Each system is tested on the level of structure and scale and on the level of constructive expression and decorative arbitrariness. Christian Hauvette chooses a code in continual renewal because any architectural sign is at least double. It cannot be merely that which it is; for example, cement can evoke stone, or wood, or marble, or canvas, or tissue or textiles. Architectural space is encumbered with objects and signs carrying evocations, which overlap and arrange themselves in a language that is doubly articulated. In this way, architecture reveals that which in construction mocks the possibility of complicity, exploiting the confusion between the object and the knowledge we believe we have of it.

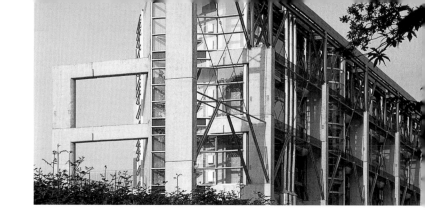

Regional Audit House, Britanny
(classic signature, technique)

6 | Tribute

Architecture pays a heavy tribute to the dominant system of representation. Representation, or as one might say in this period of late capitalism (an era of consumer plug-ins, the euphoria of a life syncopated by the generalized excitement produced by continual rotations and reconfigurations of objects, of appearances, of images, all turned into objects of merchandise), actualized *revolving* representation. To revolve, to turn, to play a trick, take one's turn and come back. And, by extension, "revolver": akin to an efficient tool for killing, which releases a projectile, rapidly, then another, and so on and on. A "revolving/revolver representation" – orbiting the etymological suggestion – can only conceive of signs as ephemeral, possessing a very brief life span. Allied to fashion and to the imperative of continual change, this "revolving/revolver representation" can only occasionally fall back on the systems of stable signs, dominant in the classical age and late into the capitalistic system arising from the industrial revolution: beauty, composition, equilibrium for the classics; ugliness and decomposition, unity of the medium, autonomy or radicalism for the moderns. To these (the stable signs), "revolving/revolver representation" prefers *meta-signs*: citations, clever allusions, kitsch in whatever the current formula may be, and clichés, which, as we all know, are always based on consensus, quickly swallowed, and – as quickly – digested.

As it grapples with the "revolving/revolver representation" (the neo-modernist movement) architecture generally cuts a pitiful figure. First of all by its material servitude: this is the poverty of the architect whose studio barely gets by if it is not constantly fashionable, and sweating hard to decide whom to kill or resurrect next. And further by the facile nature of its methods: the poverty of these showy principles, centered excessively on the instantaneously contemporary (the need to be "in"), the greatest glory of which is in stimulating stupidity: the blind stupidity of the followers, always ready to catch whatever train is leaving the platform; the calculated stupidity of politicians for whom such projects instantaneously magnify the public décor, symbolic validation of the crass mediocrity that is the daily conduct of current affairs. Hauvette's architecture replies to this system of values – or non-values – on three levels: distance, technique, and doubt. 1 – Distance: any building by Christian Hauvette frankly declares its distance from extreme contemporary "vibrations," refusing unconditional adherence to them (his "classical imprint" which, rightly, is so often evoked). More than in terms of style, this attitude of distance should be interpreted as a question of basic principles, as an ethical position. As a rampart against frenetic activity, it is the position from which today's infatuations can be perceived for what, in most cases they truly are: periodic fevers in the history of the West, which loves to see itself in a state of constant convulsion. 2 – Technique: technological constraints are important to Hauvette. A building for him is not the unleashing of an imaginary object. He rejects the idea of raw inspiration, of the primacy of a romantic disposition, of the imperative need for symbolic citation. The mechanics of form result less from an esthetic project than from preliminary constraints, both material and, above all, technical.[7] Material necessity, as Hauvette says, can play the role of a stop (an abutment), seeing a form emerge, which does not conform to the continuums of which the building should in principle be the fervent ally: topographic continuum in the urban space, stylistic continuum in respect of the dominant architectural esthetic, etc. This echoes the lesson of Jean Prouvé, under whom Hauvette studied, a lesson which underlines the importance of an organic esthetic which the structural element codifies. 3 – Doubt: here the architect says it best: "*If there is a counterpoint to my system, it's that I often ask myself where architecture is. You never know when it is going to appear, and this is terrible.*"[8]

**Fountain of Lafayette
Polytechnic School**
(theater without
spectacle)

7,9 | Effects, theatre

The result is an architecture, which is not estranged but present, more coherent than stylized, more structured than integrated. No dramatic surprises, no melodramatic effects violently thrust into the theater of urban forms, but something different – a vitality. Form that is both self-sufficient and active, gifted with its own energy, creating its own expansive space without – for all that – pushing for autonomy (the building as lighthouse) nor oozing into the local tissue like a pustule (the building as canker, as turd, as raw stuff, ejected or thrown up in haste).

Architecture is a mute but noisy theater. It's a stage for hysterics, where one plays with volumes before playing with words, where one struts not with deadly ripostes but with delirious principles, carnival elevations, and gratuitous technical virtuosity totally divorced from usage. This scene is comparable to those inherent in the arts of the stage, such as: striking a pose, exhibitionism, demonstrative but weak volition, and the desire to perform. With Christian Hauvette architecture rediscovers, if not its theatrical virginity, then at least the legitimacy of play through the calculated manner in which he negates theatrical effects, pulling out all the stops. The literary effect in architecture is a case in point. "Literary effect?" See Tatlin's the "*Monument to the Third International*:" a habitable, three-dimensional copy of Marx's theories on the realized revolution (a work that will no more be built than the true Marxist revolution was ever *realized* – another pipe dream, come to life on paper only). Yet another example is the *Tucker House* by Venturi and Rauch: this is a synthesis of Goethe's bourgeois gazebo and of the cabin in the woods to which pioneers of the "american experience," from London to Kerouac, retire their bodies sated with the thousand experiences of promiscuity. To break the "literary effect," in this fashion, Hauvette re-evokes all the mythologies and reveals their cathartic character; a lesson learned from Roland Barthes, another of his professors. A building doesn't write or tell a story or history, be it a history of glory, of alienation, or of pain. Above all, it is, in synthesis, its own story. Equally, the "cinematic effect" is banished. None of that reversal, become so frequent in 20th Century architecture: the art of building soon defined itself by its privileged relationship to the invention of the Lumière brothers; it was soon tempted to mimic the cinema, multiplying effects of sequence and montage, coloured frames, and kinetic treatments. In terms of modeled images, far from this appetite for transforming real architecture, in the end, into the equivalent of film décor, Hauvette's architecture offers something much more meaningful than that which is hidden. In his architecture not everything is evident. You have to look at the details, you have to look more closely, you have to admit the existence of subtle devices which do not produce an immediate effect: the use of the trade wind in the Education Authority of Martinique; the deceptive simplicity of the fountain of the Lafayette Polytechnic School, which, when activated, will produce a rainbow at certain hours of the day; the enigmatic huts on the flat roofs of the two apartment towers in Rennes, which create the impression that the building has been left unfinished, arousing a curiosity that cannot be satisfied.

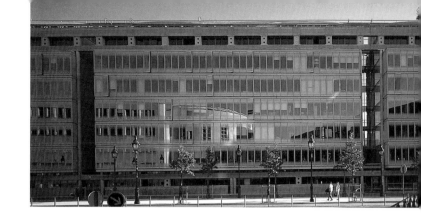

Headquarters of the
French Development
Agency, Paris,
12th arrondissement
(truth in construction)

8 | Architectural efficacy

The work of architecture, it is assumed, is enclosed by a meaning, created by an intention. It tries to be a totality, complete, closed, and possessing a core. This core, it is assumed, is the substance of architecture. Architecture therefore would have the mission of guiding us towards this ultimate treasure, which we should admire and contemplate.

This notion has evoked two reactions, two very lively, caricature-like responses. On the one hand, it is said that there is no core, that architecture is merely space traversed by continually cross-referenced meanings. This is the reign of architecture as a palimpsest, held prisoner by an esthetic of chaos, fascinated by the geometric and formal complexity that it produces. On the other hand, it is said that we must return to this lost core, and thus become imprisoned in copying models of the past, in academic formalism. The resulting architecture suffers from formal redundancy, from an obsession with facades, citations, from a cortege of false marble, false frontons, false colonnades, etc.

In both cases, the ultimate treasure quickly reveals itself to be no more than a discourse laden with esoteric references; its meaning dissolved, all it leaves behind, as residue, is the esthetic phenomenon it has engendered.

Christian Hauvette systematically strips away all these attempts to have recourse to ultimate foundations: in a sense, he destroys the myths of origins, eliminates the fog created by total explanations. Yes, architecture is built on a phenomenon of moving away from the core, of de-centering. Creation arises from a conflict between diverse meanings, the synthesis of which often appears improbable at first. The sign is opaque; it demolishes the interpretive illusion. At the same time, architecture is in search of efficacy: "*At the beginning of a project I think in terms of construction. I call that 'in truth.' If I had to philosophize, I'd say that I am interested in the problem of certainty. Is it possible in a project to define a series of certain elements, which from that point on can be combined as in the play with elements of a language? Something which is certain, is something which is identified, that's to say, both correctly sectioned and correctly constructible. It's something that disposes, as an element, of a limited range of interpretations.*"[9] One must eliminate the

"static" in architecture (metaphors used as discursive and commercial alibis, the codes of façadism and of ornamentation) and isolate what is constant: solidity, materiality; the events that animate architecture and create its uses; the imaginary constants that assure that the building will never be reduced to its strict functionality nor merely to the uses set forth in the plan.

These constants are treated like structural layers. Architecture according to Christian Hauvette shows both a presence and an absence; it reveals a facade but it suggests that there are other things to discover:
– The facade on the Seine side of the building for the Savings and Loans Bank (1998-completion 2002) is a glass sheet pierced by a luminous slit that signals the presence of an internal street. The effect creates a density, it makes a thickness visible, and this intensifies the imaginative dimension of the building.

– The facade on the side facing the square of the building of the French Development Agency (1994-98) breaks with the principle of linear alignment, and dissolves into triangular blocks, each displaced in relation to the others, thus creating a series of angles and shadows. Each block of the building is suspended from a concrete beam, which crowns it, and which is left visible at the extreme end of the facade. This approach to construction creates a great freedom in the glazed mass of the facade, rhythm through the movement of the etched glass doors and windows. The de-boxed system of the triangular blocks of the facade is echoed in the interior arrangement of the office spaces.

One might say that the efficacy of architecture, its constructive truth, comes precisely from the equilibrium that is maintained between the correspondences (of materials: glass, concrete, steel; of colors: grays, bluish tinges; of relations between proportions of the interior and exterior elements – the height of the facade's supporting beam is equal to the height of the ground floor) and the differences (in layout: triangular blocks of decreasing dimensions, adapted to the shape of the site; asymmetry of the lighting panels). Christian Hauvette evades the trap of the interpretive illusion by revealing the rules of his architecture and the effects of their relationships.

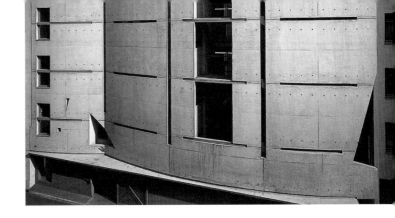

Nursery in the rue
Saint-Maur, Paris,
11th arrondissement
(metaphor, play)

10 | Play

Christian Hauvette's architecture hides intelligent play that aims at subverting modernist codes, transforming buildings into objects that are "brutal and polemic": the mysterious openings in the raw concrete facade of the nursery in the rue Saint-Maur (1986-90), and the reinterpretation of the monumental figure via the immense yard of the Lafayette Polytechnic School in Clermont-Ferrand (1988-91), a real-false ellipse, where the architectural form no longer corresponds to this *"indecipherable package, this preemptory and indigestible sculptural mass, which the architect is supposed to get his public to swallow."*[10] Architectural material – it's not this homogeneous paste, this unitary mask that it is so often considered to be. In fact, one should rather speak of a "system of architecture," in the sense of those analyses developed by Roland Barthes to deal with literature or fashion: it is no longer a question of simply organizing signs among themselves but of finding a position between a clarity of energy (the efficacy of architecture) and a force of invention (creating an obstacle to the desires of the financiers and the users). Buildings are aggressive games played with or against languages, against codes, and aim at eliminating everything that can make the "paste" seem homogeneous: or lend it legitimacy by way of beauty, truth, or a linear history.

The risk is great. There may be an infraction of the rules. The game may be obscure: *"My friends make fun of my buildings which at first they consider very ugly… Basically, it's true because they really don't look like what people expected of them. They are neither very showy nor very fashionable."*[11] Architecture thus freed from all decorative effects can take the time to engage in a game of unlimited interactions based on experimenting with systems of opposites. By this, Christian Hauvette thwarts the discourse of single meanings, unilateral classification, and determinations. Architecture remains a source of astonishment. Interpretation is never complete. It is rather like those tarot games in Italo Calvino's tale of *The Castle of Crossed Destinies*: *"It's the metaphor of 'jumping to the side,' the moment the building escapes me, detours away from my intentions. Our world would not be livable without this power of 'indirection' coming – not from the subject – but from the object itself."*[12]

The game lies in the difference. The difference is founded on the openness of the work. When it is born, the work differentiates itself from its creator and also from the rest of the world. The work differentiates itself from its original reference. The metaphor, for example, which the architect uses as a provisional game in the construction of the project, is of 'raw material' that strives towards an end which is not yet explicit. *"It's a question of not confusing one's inductive principle – an efficient tool, but reserved for private use – with the persuasive mechanism it inevitably becomes upon exhibition."*[13] At the same time, the work opens up to other imaginary spaces, to other languages – to mechanics or music, for example: not in order to reproduce their form, but to remain in contact with everything that surrounds it, to preserve an opening, a horizon. The work of architecture is a source of wonder, of questioning before the world and society. Thus, the game is founded not only on original differences but also on their continued existence.

1 Michel Serres, *Les origines de la géométrie*, Flammarion, 1993, pp. 211 to 214.
2 Ibid.
3 Christian Hauvette, *Suite … sans fin*, collection Ombre vive, Jeanne-Marie Sens and Hubert Tonka, Pandora editions, 1991, p. 9.
4 François Lamarre, *Le bestiaire de Christian Hauvette*, in "L'Empreinte," June 1999, No. 45, p. 34.
5 Chantal Béret, *Architectures en mouvement*, in *1989*. Éditions du Regard, Paris, 1995, p. 269.
6 Robert Venturi, Complexity and Contradiction in Architecture, MOMA, 2nd edition, 1990, p. 23.
7 For a more detailed discussion see Marie-Hélène Contal's analysis in *Christian Hauvette*, éditions Gustavo Gili, Barcelona-Mexico, 1997, introduction, p. 10.
8 Christian Hauvette, interview in *extra-ordinary*, No. 1, In-Ex projects/Paris & Birkhäuser – Publishers for Architecture/ Basel, Boston, Berlin, 1999, p. 175.
9 Christian Hauvette, ibid., p. 170.
10 Christian Hauvette, *Croiseur Lumière, Ecole nationale Louis Lumière, Etats des lieux*, les éditions du Demi-Cercle, 1989, p. 17.
11 Christian Hauvette, interview in *In-Ex*, issue 1, p. 169.
12 Christian Hauvette, ibid., p. 175.
13 Denis Pondruel, *Christian Hauvette*, collection Gros Plan, IFA, 1994, p. 7.

204 HOUSING UNITS PARIS
40 HOUSING UNITS RENNES
166 HOUSING UNITS RENNES

Foundations

Denis Pondruel

Reading again the texts on artist Absalon, who constructed cells of a kind, I am intrigued by the term "monolith" which the author employs to qualify the work. The same qualifier is contained in Paul Virilio's writing on the subject of bunkers.

In both cases the observers emphasize that what strikes them most is the absence of foundation. Indeed, to their eyes the absence best characterizes this type of construction and from it they deduce, for the one and for the other, a kind of autonomy that extends as far as to evoke a nomadic sense.

Hence the interest in examining this question of autonomy in architecture. But looking at it in broader strokes, more revealing than the simply architectural autonomy evoked by Virilio. In other words, since the foundation is linked with the ground one would do well to explore that which, no less effectively, provides a link between object and the symbolic, aesthetic, and ideological context.

This throws up once again the question of the object as rhetorical machine and of its necessary use when a new object is to be inscribed on a site. Simpler still, it gives rise to the problem of the inevitable presentation of specifications and the metaphoric narratives needed to convince (the authorities) and to obtain the construction permit.

It all boils down to the question of connection.

Connection to the ground, to reality, to the tangible, to whatever else I know!

To something that is already acknowledged.

And then, returning to it a second time, the question becomes: can one get rid of the connections once the project has been accepted? For truly, one dreams of getting rid of them and of escaping from the enforced conformity they impose.

Were it possible to rid oneself of them, the building might attain a far more interesting kind of autonomy than the strictly mechanical one suggested in the beginning.

In Christian Hauvette's architecture there is an example which, I believe, demonstrates both this desire and its implementation: the 166 housing units built for a private developer in 1996 in Rennes.

A style in two beats and two buildings.

First building

Right away one is struck by the intricacy of this construction. The rigor of the concept serves as symbol, while at the same time making it accessible. One could say that this building is founded on a complex network of specificities and cultural virtues with elegance and precision at the forefront. If it weren't such a hackneyed idea, I would say that it is founded on a particularly French sense of proportion; I am thinking of Diderot or Rameau. An elegance that is linked to performance without showing off, yet calculated with precision, and connected to a certain weightlessness of shapes that is pure ideology: to mathematical agility. All this relates so closely to "values," that one cannot resist being convinced – gradually, as it were – by the quality of the whole. As if a kind of contiguity of qualities were at work.

Here then are the true foundations, which make this a building that is solidly attached to the ground, thus immovable.

So connected, in fact, and not only to the geological but also to the ideological, esthetic and moral context, that it becomes the opposite of a nomadic building.

These are all likable and defendable qualities. In my view, (however) too much on the side of argumentation, legitimatization, estheticism and communication.

Then comes the moment when it all takes off.

Second building

Having designed one of the fine buildings that are his trade-mark, Hauvette envisioned crowning this elegant structure with a kind a squared spud, an object two stories high whose exterior is reminiscent of the types of shacks found on construction sites. To complete the gesture, he wanted to cover the parallelepiped in red shale. This cladding would have alluded to and completed the atrocious decor of an adjoining maisonette, a bar called "chez Brigitte."

In parody of the duty of integration? Of treating continuities to the letter?

The load was too heavy and provoked a general outcry from the sponsors.

After much debate, Hauvette was forced to yield and use a copper facing for the parallelepiped instead.

Nevertheless, the essential statement was saved: the ridiculous Lego remained, unjustifiable.

Now then, the casual monolith comes into view.

It is unlike anything and insists upon nothing. It is without quality. And yet this near-archaic Dionysian hut is supported by the most refined and most solidly rooted base imaginable. The fact is that this "grotesque" is enhanced and elevated by a built volume that could pass for the very embodiment of quality and dignity.

The urbanity of the one is but a foil for the savage nature of the other.

To justify a building in this grotesque manner would be the same as not justifying it at all, mimicking the very procedure of justification and the absurd functioning of negotiation. Such assertive integration stirs the contrary: maliciously, a wave is set free which – through denial – shows the building in the process of liberating itself from its foundations. A building that reaches autonomy to this degree simultaneously attains a much more complex register, one that has much in common with a work of art. This ontological leap is only possible as a result of clever maneuvers, feints and dodges. There really is something of a Laclos in the dear architect.

This apartment building rises next to the Paris ring road, considered in the zoning regulations as a main urban boulevard like any other. The building is thus placed along side a curved slip-road that regulates access. The architecture articulates two distinct programs or functions in two distinct blocks: family apartments below, bachelor/intern apartments above. To the south, and seen from the family apartments, the spectacle of passing traffic contrasts with the silence created by the "acoustic" facade. This thick, polished concrete wall shelters the kitchens and the living rooms behind long glazed bays. Two layers of glazing are separated by sixty centimeters. The space between accommodates a blind and the air-conditioning system. Exterior gangways painted in blue provide access to the bachelor units on the upper levels. Between these two sections an empty "deck" articulates the scintillating concrete and the blue of the ring road, a terrace overlooking the Parisian horizon.

Project Team
Architect: Christian Hauvette

Client
Société Nationale Immobilière

Developer
SCIC-AMO

Project
96 family apartments and 105 bachelor apartments for employees of the Ministry of the Interior (with 204 parking spaces for the police forces)

Floor area: 12,150 m^2
Cost: 73 million francs (before tax)
Cost per m^2: 6,000 francs (before tax)/m^2
Completion: January 1995

204 Housing Units

Paris, 18th arrondissement 1991▪1995

The building is erected on a parcel near the Parisian ring road, on the suburban side at the height of the porte de la Chapelle. The 100-m facade runs parallel to the ring road whose noise levels reach 100 decibels.

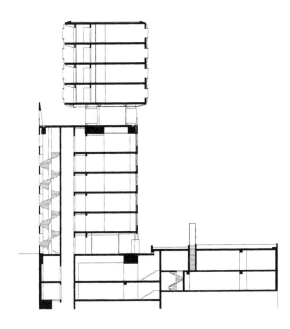

Section of building
showing the gap in
the upper volume,
a nod to the tradition
of recessed volumes
on Parisian boulevards

Scale 1:500

The facade of the lower section of the building, like skittles in polished black concrete, accommodates the service installations for the air-conditioning system. Each housing unit has a large, 6-m-wide south-facing window through which daylight pours into the living room and the kitchen.

The facades and gables are articulated with metal fire escapes.

A facade in gray concrete overlooks the turnaround at the Impasse Marteau, a cul-de-sac linked to the ramp that leads to the ring road.

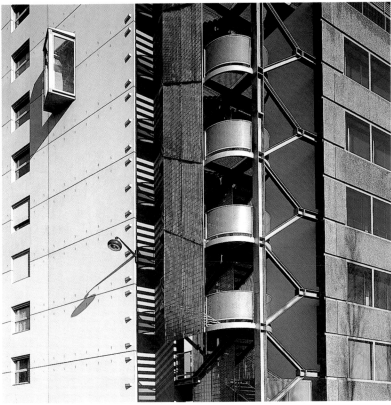

The majority of the housing units follow a front to back layout, with living
room and kitchen systematically arranged facing south and bedrooms
to the north where they are sheltered from the noise.

The openings onto the ring road are double-glazed, the external frame fixed and the internal frame sliding. A venetian blind is set into the space between the two frames. A sliding glass door separates the living room from the kitchen.

page 26/27
A promenade bridge runs like a balcony along the sixth floor.
It divides the family units on the first five floors from the bachelor units
on the seventh to tenth floors. Access to this autonomous block
is provided by vertical shafts set at the two extremities of the slab.

A complementary emergency staircase provides access
to the connecting sections of the residence.

The structural frame of the upper block differs from that of the lower volume, resulting in a load transfer on the promenade bridge level.

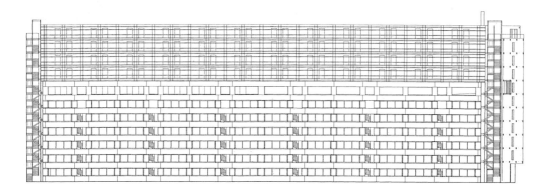

South elevation
Scale 1:750

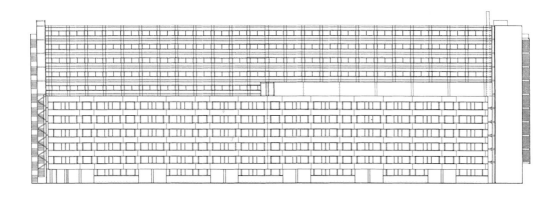

North elevation
Scale 1:750

Floor plan of family units,
1st to 5th floor

Floor plan of bachelor
units, 7th to 10th floor

Scale 1:750

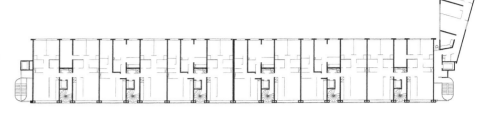

The importance of public transportation in urban peripheries provides the argument for these two "modules" which are perfectly adapted to modern life. The two small towers in rough concrete, raised on feet and encircled in aluminum, each accommodate twenty apartments. Cars and surfboards can be parked on the ground floor beneath the pillars.
A scarlet bonnet designates the entrance halls without ambiguity.
The facades are without balconies, but merely large windows whose sliding shutters of perforated aluminum filter artificial and natural light.

Project Team
Architect: Christian Hauvette
Associate architects: Cabinet B.N.R.

Client
Aiguillon Construction

Program
40 apartments for social housing

Floor area: 2,888 m²
Cost: 10,9 million francs (before tax)
Cost per m²: 3,775 francs (before tax)/m²
Completion: January 1996

40 Housing Units

Rennes 1992 ▪ 1996

Model built to exemplify useable space

Floor plan of a ground floor
unit on pilotis, with entrance
hall and several recesses,
and of a standard floor
with two 3-room units and two
2-room units

Scale 1:400

The two buildings are identical in plan, the one on the right is simply pivoted by 90 degrees with regard to the other. The client named this block of social housing units after "Paul Verlaine."

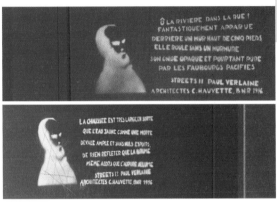

Reading again Paul Verlaine's complete works,
the architect sought to find a poem that could be
used for the building's name which he had not chosen
and which could then be graffitied in the entrance
halls in the manner of Ernest Pignon-Ernest.

Ô la rivière dans la rue !
Fantastiquement apparue
Derrière un mur haut de cinq pieds,
Elle roule sans un murmure,
Son onde opaque et pourtant pure,
Par les faubourgs pacifiés.

La chaussée est très large, en sorte
Que l'eau jaune comme une morte
Dévale ample et sans nuls espoirs
De rien refléter que la brume,
Même alors que l'aurore allume
Les cottages jaunes et noirs.

Paul Verlaine, **Streets II**, Aquarelles

Streets II

A river in the street!
Dream apparition
Flowing soundless
Behind a five-foot wall.
Dark yet still pure tide
Threading the quiet town.

The road's so wide
That death-yellow water spreads
Unable to reflect
More than fog
Though dawn lights
Black and yellow houses up.

[In a new translation by Martin
Sorrell from the Oxford World's
Classics series, "Paul Verlaine,
Selected Poems", 1999, p. 93]

The small sliding shutter in delicately perforated
lacquered aluminum provides shelter for the bedrooms.
The large, and more transparent shutter provides
shade for the living rooms.

In the center of town the banks of the river Vilaine and the Café Brigitte are nostalgic places, which the city of Rennes plans to preserve. And the plot size offers a wonderful opportunity to create a true urban oasis around a large rectangular park.

The "Brigitte" house provided an argument for crowning the project. It has been multiplied on the rooftops in the shape of red copper-covered volumes surrounded by large patios.

The first six floors are sheltered from the street by continuous balconies protected against rain and sunshine by white awnings, automatically controlled by a series of anemometers.

On the garden side, large prefabricated window boxes in polished concrete create a planted border.

Project Team
Architect: Christian Hauvette
Associate architects: Cabinet B.N.R.
Landscape architect: Alexandre Chemetoff

Client
Ocodim – Giboire Immobilier

Developer
S 2 R, Société Rennaise de Renovation

Program
166 apartments for owner-occupation
(with 268 underground parking spaces)

Floor area: 11,267 m^2
Cost: 51 million francs (before tax)
Cost per m^2: 4,525 francs (before tax)/m^2
Completion: October 1996

166 Housing Units

Rennes 1992 ▪ 1996

The urban islet would be perfectly regular if the "Café Brigitte" hadn't resisted the developer's campaign, refusing to sell its parcel.

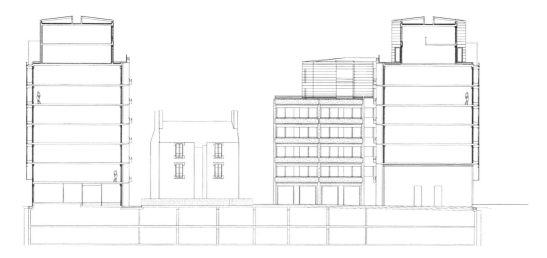

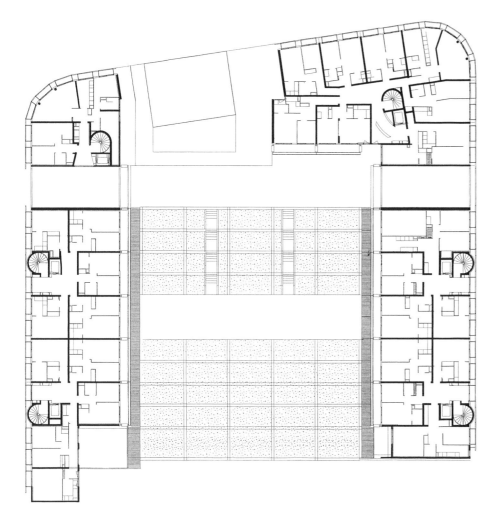

The individual houses are bedecked
in copper whose colour is reminiscent
of the red shale gables characteristic
of 19th century buildings in the Rennes
region.

Facing the road, the standard floors of the building are encircled by continuous 60-cm-wide balconies. Each bay window is outfitted with a classic blind, doubled on the balcony by a retractable awning on metal guides. Each awning is motorized and linked to an anemometer which controls its automatic retraction in strong winds (to the right of the picture). Thus there are two ways of shading each room: one across the entire facade, the other partial on the exterior.

The seventh and eighth floors are taken
up by individual duplex units set opposite
one another; each is provided with
a large outdoor patio. The apartments
on the lower levels feature balconies
with reinforced concrete elements filled
with top soil.

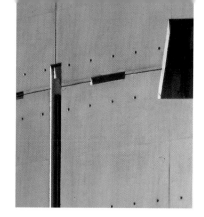

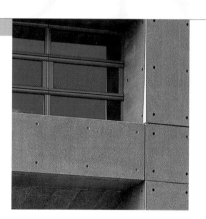

NURSERY FOR 80 CHILDREN PARIS
LAFAYETTE POLYTECHNIC SCHOOL CLERMONT-FERRAND
BRANCH OFFICE FOR THE FRENCH DEVELOPMENT AGENCY PARIS
OFFICE BUILDING FOR THE SAVINGS AND LOANS BANK PARIS

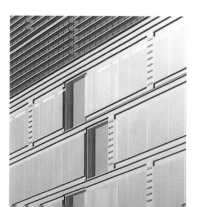

Awaiting the Monument

Didier Laroque

In ancient times, the word "patrimony" implied a legal and political certainty that has become foreign to us. It was tied to objects to which duration gave a patina of truth. These objects embodied civilization. They provided an outward expression for one's innermost longings. They provided a tool of persuasion against violent onslaught, a means of questioning certain assumptions. The civilized object, which we will refer to as the monument and which constitutes our patrimony, compels us to strive for knowledge, thus fulfilling ourselves as human beings. This is the principle, which drives a community to develop a code of ethics – the foundation of any community, its essential expression.

"In fact," writes Baldine Saint Girons, "deriving as it does from the Latin word *moneo*, causative of the root *men* (to think), the monument induces thought. It is inward meaning, memory as well as warning, strong suggestion as well as simple word of advice, transfer, and the holding of breath. *Monitor* refers to the prompter (*moniteur*), whose role it is to compensate for any loss of memory, but he also is someone who guides, who instructs. A monument inspires. It is the source of all breath, symbolizing the life of the intellect, forever enduring."

Within the monument lies the knowledge of what it faces, the foundation of the city; αρετή, the attribute of the nobleman, nobility itself, the basic tenets of all aristocratic teachings in Ancient Greece, combining courage and morality – moral beauty, which would become *virtus*. All this is implied in the term monument, which has been forgotten, quite forgotten.

As ecologically-driven associations and political parties are formed and are taken more and more seriously, we see a loathing of the monument, a fear of having sinned against the spirit by considering the earth as something to exploit rather than as a living mother. From this stems the uncomfortable feeling of having turned all of creation against itself. Increasingly, we witness cities and countryside turning into funeral pyres. The most basic of ecological concerns can be stated in very clear terms: "Are we capable of seeing the world as an intelligible idea?"

Antoine Picon likens modern cities to the worlds portrayed in electronic games, tailor-made for a creature that is a cross between a man and a machine. He writes: "Equipped from childhood with an assortment of technical gadgets, identified and controlled by systems that regulate his health, his career and his bank accounts, the citizen of a developed nation begins to resemble a cyborg." This creature embodies the horror of what

Heidegger identifies as technique. It also resembles the statue of the beast referred to in the apocalypse. The rise of technique places man in an apocalyptic world where he has convinced himself that he is nothing more than a machine.

In recent years, there have been a number of publications dealing with land art, landscape, and garden art. Still, the discussion has for the most part remained at the lofty level of generalization, even though theories have proliferated and have found their niche. As things stand, no study has posed the fundamental question of composition in an effort to illuminate the meaning of landscape – that is, an examination of the ornamental dimension.

As civilization progresses, the ornament does not recede (as was the belief of the followers of Loos): the ornament *is* the civilization, it embodies it.
The ornament can be seen as laying the foundation of the locus.

If one is ignorant of the art of the past, it is impossible to recognize what is of interest in the present. Anyone who undertakes a serious study of ancient works of art will realize that a monument must do more than merely document – and will indeed be aware that its historical nature is of no particular significance. Any individual, any nation, indifferent to this awareness cannot claim to be civilized. One of the main responsibilities of the state as well as of the individual is to stream education towards what is supremely intelligible – insofar as this represents the common good and becomes the common thread that binds any community.

Many of this century's architects unwittingly shared the same desire for self-destruction, exemplified in their hatred of the monument. They saw it as an expression of a boundary, something obstructing the human will, a sign that the individual was subjugated to the State or to religion. They refused to admit that any boundaries existed. This is why the modern city seems to imply the collapse of the soul. What we find is a deep-seated antagonism towards all that transpires the canons of western european civilization, a fascination with degradation and death.

It seems obvious that modern architecture has made a pact with death, with its little sister, fashion. Architects have taken a perverse pleasure in their own abasement, in seeing spirit gradually being bled from architecture. In no longer being architects. In making sure that architecture is no longer monumental.

Concerns about monumentality are increasingly present in Hauvette's projects and works. The Regional Chamber of Finance of Brittany, completed in 1988, strives for a classical feel through a systematic organization of pilasters, linked by a double beam; the design of a college built in 1991 and dedicated to Clermont-Ferrand is inspired by a Roman amphitheater; a portico has been added to the Education Authority at the Academy of the West Indies and Guyana, built three years later; the French Development Agency, the main branch of the French Development Bank in Paris, seems to be organized as a series of pylons. In his most recent project, along the Seine near the gare d'Austerlitz train station, Hauvette's quest for monumentality is imbued with an inner sense, refusing to draw attention to itself. He seems to be moving towards a simplicity in his architecture which embraces the abstract, an endeavor which is unprecedented. Abstraction is the purest expression of monumentality. The visual arts are a fine example of this.

If, upon viewing an abstract work of art, one is sometimes left with the feeling of having been duped, this is surely due to the fact that it appears to have been produced without any effort. The techniques involved in producing a monochrome, for instance, seem rather basic. How can one be impressed by a work which, it would seem, could be carried out by practically anyone? Should it then surprise us when, upon realizing that this meagre accomplishment has been legitimized through intellectual, official or commercial channels, someone reacts with disbelief, even hostility?
Art as practiced in the past seems difficult to achieve. In this context, any claim to producing something worthy of the name of art is contingent upon mastering a proper technique. Accordingly, one of the conditions for creating a work of art would be to impose a formal constraint on the creative process. It is believed that art begins with technique. This may be debatable.

Of all of Hauvette's previously mentioned work, the main branch of the French Development Agency seems to best exemplify this expectancy of looking for the monument. We will hereby give a brief description of the building and its site, in order to demonstrate in practical terms how the architect's mental hand carries out its work.

In Paris, the cluster of buildings in the Châlons area, which spreads its squalor and ruin at the foot of the gare de Lyon, is now a thing of the past. The quarter has been entirely rebuilt around a town square somewhat reminiscent of the Piazza del Campo in Sienna. Many urban planners are feeble-minded, perhaps the vast majority of them. These days, the art of designing cities, squares, appears to have gone by the wayside. Utilitarianism and profit, as well as ignorance seem to form the basis of many urban planners' decisions. It is high time to apply an artistic vision to city planning. The square at Châlons, and it goes without saying, is in dire need of a dose of myth-making. What exists now is certainly far superior to what was there before – it is no great feat to improve on sordidness. What is missing, however, is something that reflects the unity and dignity of the city.

From this vantage point, one gets a side view of Christian Hauvettes building. It seems to impose itself on the square. It stands out as an island of stillness and emotion in an atonal, dis-jointed mass, a thing that appears both distracted and con-cerned, made even drearier by a busy road that passes further down, all of this a living testament to the shortage of funds that led to poor maintenance of roads and urban fixtures. This new building, which seems placed at the tip of this quarter, is none other than the main branch of the French Development Bank, a state bank.

The bank is designed as a system of five separate volumes where the triangular planes provide each office facing south, towards the tracks, equal amounts of sunlight and a clear view. A tradi-tional comb-like arrangement would give an obstructed view, allowing for less transparency. The structure, supported by a thick concrete beam, is painstakingly drawn, remarkable for its sharpness and elegance. It has an overall appearance of seriousness and complexity. Its exterior as well as its interior certainly make this one of the least conventional office build-ings in Paris. The extended interior arcade which joins the five sections of the design and is punctuated by shafts of light, the volumes of the entrance and the connecting passages on the ground floor, the large restaurant area all display a certain flare and are suffused with soft light. Thanks to its design, future occupants of the building can expect a less dwarfed existence than their counterparts at the Défense or at the Front de Seine, where the surroundings induce moral depletion, discouraging anyone from feeling anything, shrouding them in a great pall of weariness. Hauvette's multifaceted design elicits the exact opposite response.

Here, architectural design is life-affirming. It tells a story where quite distinct geometric structures, sometimes at odds with one another, coalesce, and begin to converse with one another. Generally speaking, Hauvette's work sets into motion eloquent conversations between separate architectural systems.

Amongst architects, Hauvette is not of the changeable type, whose trademark is to entertain vague hopes and who is easily swayed by the insistance of a powerful client or a large-scale company bent on limiting his vision to small enclosures, to sentimental dabblings, or even to reduce him to silence. In its context and within careful boundaries, the main branch of the Development Agency makes an eloquent case for what is meant by "awaiting the monument."

It is useful to note that, after obtaining his degree in architecture, Hauvette studied under Barthes, from whom he inherited a strong bent for theory which sets him apart from his colleagues and which continues to inform his writing – the prime example being his book *Suite…sans fin*, published at Éditions Pandora, Paris, 1991. Both in his writing and in his work as an architect, Hauvette values thought processes and proceeds methodically. The decisiveness of his design can be attributed to the decisiveness of his ideas. His works seem to originate in a free application of thought around what constitutes the order of architecture. His designs are rational, which explains what Hauvette means by "architectural mechanics" and which translates, in his buildings, into several systems whose association or friction with one another set up the conditions for an ordered whole. How does one tie together disparate elements? How can one orchestrate them? This is the underlying question in all of

his work. His answer echoes that of the ancients, who understood that through various interrelated proportions of a building, a vibrant and moving whole emerged. Hauvette places a lot of emphasis on regulating lines and in each one of his creations we see how clever he is at combining various levels. That which is ineffable, Hauvette holds, and can only be attained if it is not sought for; in other words, it is the by-product of an attempt to achieve something altogether different.

A true architect in some ways reaches the status of a hero. He doesn't mind being associated with false colleagues who, taking advantage of all the confusion, can be mistaken for what they definitely are not while still carrying on with an air of dignity common to swindlers who are financially viable and are never taken to task. The true architect is forced to deal with these deceivers and is often exposed to administrative wrangling. What is monumental is the struggle, lost in advance, that only courage can sustain. The monument towers above, has faith, and compels us to follow the way of intellect. The primary virtue is to be able to detect the soul's devotion and to repay it with equal faithfulness.

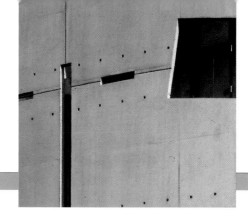

The nursery asserts itself in the neighbourhood like a "safe or stronghold" on the side that faces the road and like an open space towards the interior of the islet.

The facade of the nursery underlines the continuity in the development of the rue Saint-Maur, through both the design of its lateral "scars" and its curved front, which compensates the gap of the two adjacent buildings. The base is in response to the car exhaust that invades the capital. The raw concrete veil of the facade functions like a mask that protects the open areas in which the children romp about.

On the inside, the play areas open onto the courtyard by means of large sliding doors and balconies whose oblique glazing gives the children their first experiences of architectural vertigo.

Project Team
Architect: Christian Hauvette

Client
Direction de l'Architecture de Paris

Developer
SLA of the 11th arrondissement

Floor area: 1,281 m²
Cost: 8.9 million francs (before tax)
Cost per usable m²: 6,959 francs (before tax)/m²
Completion: May 1990

The facade on the rue Saint-Maur was constructed from concrete panels prefabricated on site in a unique frame, reused 20 times. These panels are not load-bearing; instead, they are suspended from the staircases which they mask.

NURSERY FOR 80 CHILDREN
PARIS 11ᵀᴴ ARRONDISSEMENT 1986 ⊛ 1990

The concrete beams of variable inertia and the curved false ceiling recall the curvature of the facade. The photograph at the top was taken upon completion, the image below documents the changes which usage brings to the initial esthetic.

Cross-section

Scale 1:250

At left, plan of standard floor accommodating 26 children

Scale 1:250

At right, "soft" model of the nursery in coloured silicon

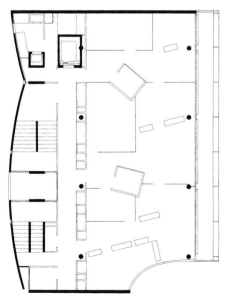

page 57
Access to hallway from the "baby safe" is effected through this unique and small sliding glass door. The hallway receives additional light through a triangular opening above.

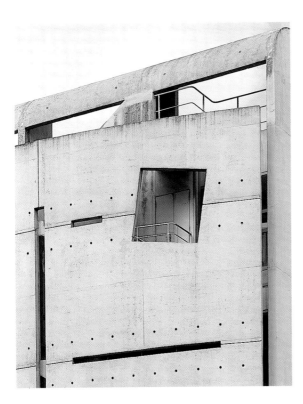

Facade on the rue Saint-Maur in 1999,
ten years after completion

Elevation on
rue Saint-Maur

Scale 1:250

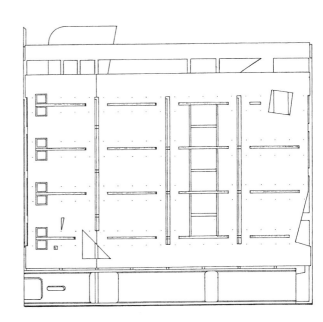

The three upper floors are identical and are intended as resting areas for the children. Sliding panels open onto glazed balconies. Play and communal activities take place on the first floor and on the ground floor, which opens onto a sheltered garden.

Elevation viewed from the garden

Scale 1:250

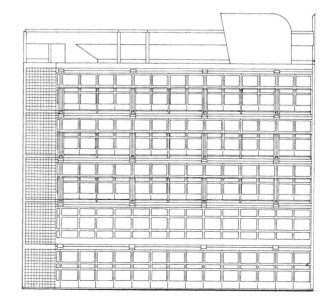

The school is located on the periphery, amidst a jumble of colorful commercial zones. Faced with this environment, this black building is conceived to dominate it through its autonomous "strength," which is readable and unitary.

The ellipse accommodates the lecture rooms and surrounds the central courtyard, a vital element in any community life. The ellipse is a symbol of permanence and rootedness, emphasizing the formal treatment of the external facade in polished concrete. The metallic and glazed skin of the internal facade, multi-faceted, creates a playful, dynamic and light side.

A large steel and aluminum bar, the so-called "wing," accommodates the wide open studio spaces. The blocks provide space for extracurricular requirements: housing, restaurant.

Project Team
Architect: Christian Hauvette
Associate architects: Atelier 4

Client
Auvergne Region

Developer
Direction Départementale de l'Equipement du Puy-de-Dôme

Floor area: 31,630 m²
Cost: 150 million francs (before tax)
Cost per m²: 4,740 francs (before tax)/m²
Completion: September 1991

Aerial view taken in October 1999, showing the different morphological elements arranged on the ground-level grid, and the planted interior courtyard

LAFAYETTE POLYTECHNIC SCHOOL
CLERMONT-FERRAND 1988 ❁ 1991

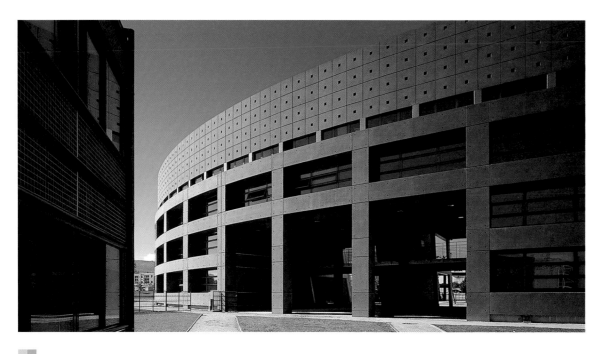

The outer wall describes a perfect ellipse. It is constructed from an interplay of posts and hollow beams in black polished concrete, whose identical section is 1,05 m by 1,05 m.

This grate serves also as a network for fluid distribution to the modular classrooms. The last floor is characterized by a more continuous layout.

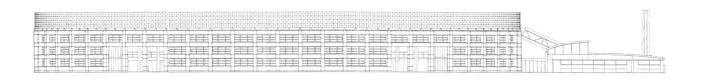

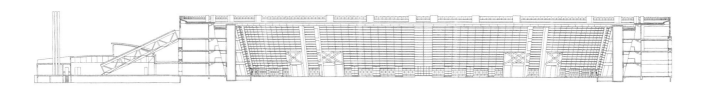

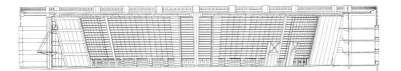

Facades and longitudinal and cross sections

Scale 1:1000

Facing page : first floor plan

Scale 1:1000

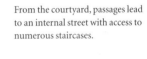

From the courtyard, passages lead to an internal street with access to numerous staircases.

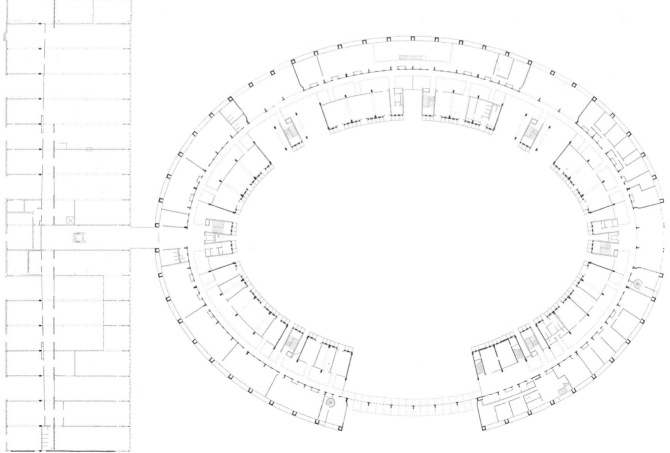

A three-story high median street is created by the space between the two structures.

The art studios occupy the uppermost level. They benefit from zenithal light.

The triangular site is located in the heart of Paris, with the south side overlooking a raised embankment for railroad tracks and the north side bordering a pedestrian boulevard.

The building for the French Development Agency is not only an office building, but also a state bank whose architecture is classic yet unpretentious.

The built development is divided into five separate elements, linked from top to bottom by a large structural portico. The gaps, which separate the five "continents," function as connecting walkways and let the rays of the sun enter into a playful dialog with the street below.

The south facade, overlooking the railroad tracks, is a series of screens, installed at variable opening angles.

The project presents five triangular, functional entities whose placement restricts the degree to which individual offices are directly opposite one another.

The volume of the first two levels occupies the whole of the site. It is connected via a longitudinal, internal street and illuminated by zenithal light through a triangular glass roof.

Project Team
Architect: Christian Hauvette
Associate architects: Atelier d'architecture
BMC

Client
Agence Française de Développement

Developer
SCET

Program
Headquarters and offices for a banking institution

Floor area: 27,000 m²
Cost: 260 million francs (before tax)
Cost per m²: 9,630 francs (before tax)/m²
Completion: April 1998

Model of the project in its environment between the mall and the raised wings of the gare de Lyon in Paris. A base fully occupies the first two levels. Ventilation ducts supply fresh air to the underground section beneath the rue de Chalon.

BRANCH OFFICE FOR THE FRENCH DEVELOPMENT AGENCY
PARIS 12TH ARRONDISSEMENT 1994❋1998

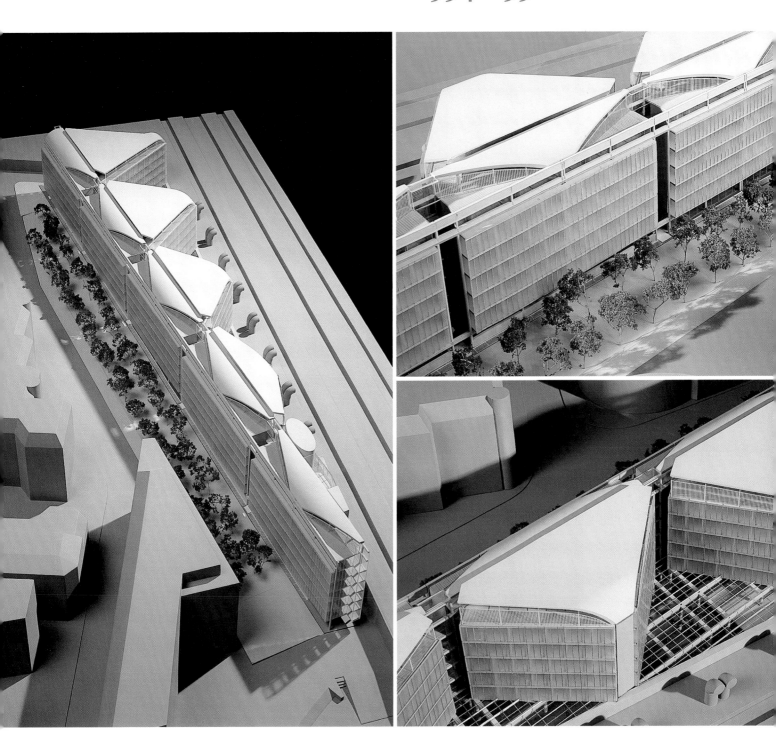

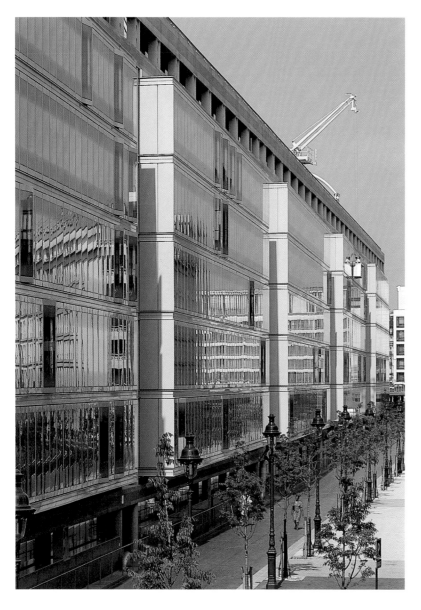

Morning (left) and evening light (facing page) on the north facade. The degree to which the facade panels open towards the outside (in the "English" manner) is limited to 11 cm.

The floors on the north facade are suspended from a concrete and steel beam that uninterruptedly spans the 200 m alongside the rue Roland Barthes.

Plans of ground
floor, first floor
and standard floor

Scale 1:1000

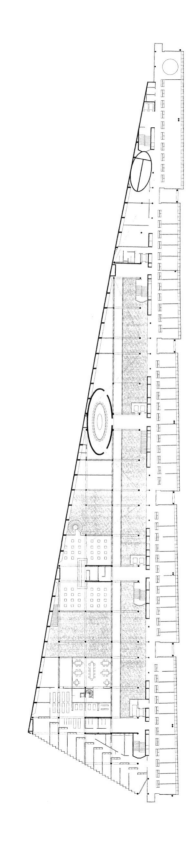

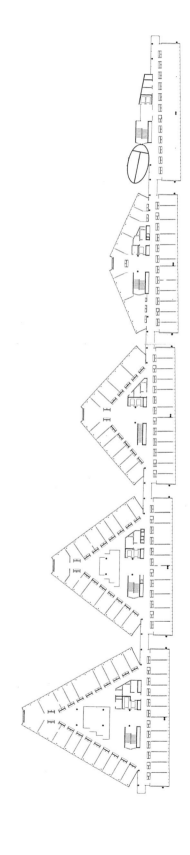

The south facade with spread-out screens overlooks the railroad tracks at 6-m-high elevation and the ventilation ducts of the subterranean maintenance road.

Cross-section
of a "strait"

1/750°

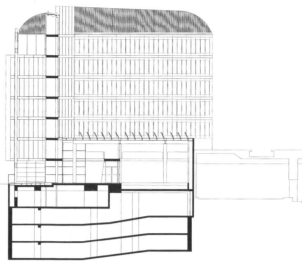

The five functional "continents" of the
building are separated by four "straits"
that create a visual link between the
north and south sections of the building.
The north facade, backlit, is brightened
by these luminous openings.

A system of sunshades protects the glass-
covered volumes in the base from direct
sunlight.

page 81
The modular desks are arranged
on a 90 cm grid. The lacquered metal
and etched glass of the panels
are completely flush with one another.

Interior views of work areas
and communal areas

A large internal street runs the length
of the building on two levels. It leads
to the elevator shafts and staircases
to each continent, as well as to all areas
in the base.

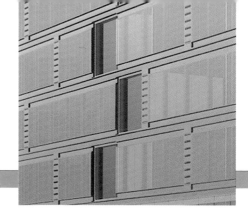

This project, in the category of "blank office spaces," proposes an urban variation on the standard typology of office buildings: a 12-m-thick bar on a 0.92 frame system, containing two rows of offices on either side of a central common area. Wrapped around the lot, this linear structure encloses a high interior nave, which opens onto the Seine and leads into the depth of the building in the manner of a Parisian mall.

The regularity of the layout is complemented by differentiated facades: sheets of glass on the north side overlooking the Seine and a jumble of glass panels on the south side facing the street. The choice of two distinct registers thwarts the "bow" effect that one anticipates from the ground. Emancipated from any symmetry, this hollow rests on a base that absorbs the slope from the riverbank to the avenue and is crowned by a black attic volume.

Project Team
Architect: Christian Hauvette

Client
Caisse des Dépôts et Consignations

Developer
SCIC Développement

Program
Registered office and offices for a banking institution

Floor area: 21,000 m²
Cost: 193 million francs (before tax)
Cost per m²: 9,190 francs (before tax)/m²
Completion: February 2002

Facade on the Seine in front
of the gare d'Austerlitz

OFFICE BUILDING FOR THE SAVINGS AND LOANS BANK
PARIS 13ᵀᴴ ARRONDISSEMENT 1998 ✶ 2002

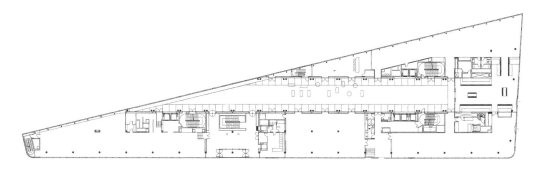

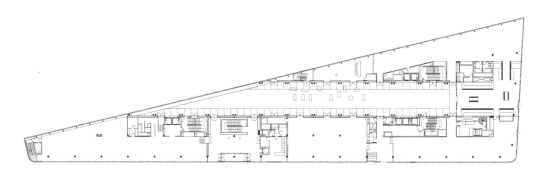

Plans of ground floor
and standard floor

Scale 1:1000

View from the new Charles de Gaulle
bridge at the intersection of the future
avenue de France

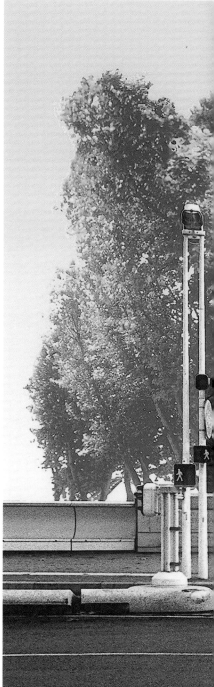

Cross section

Scale 1:500

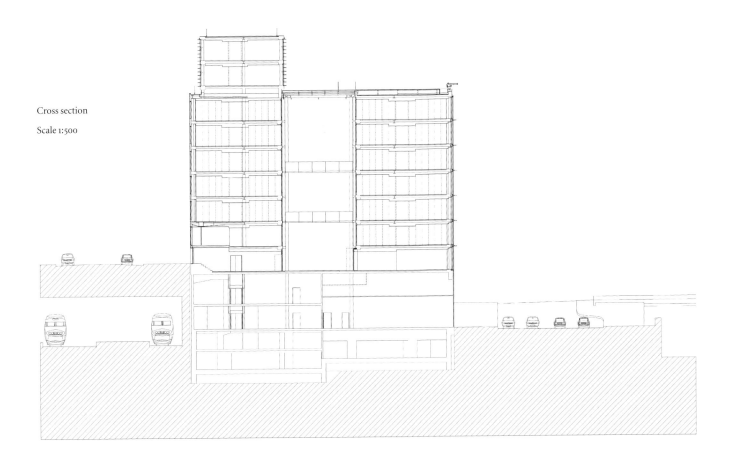

South facade on avenue de France (left)
and north facade overlooking the Seine (below)

Two views of the interior road

Following pages:
James Turrell's artistic intervention

NATIONAL COLLEGE LOUIS LUMIÈRE NOISY-LE-GRAND
EDUCATION AUTHORITY OF MARTINIQUE FORT-DE-FRANCE
RESEARCH CENTER AND SCHOOL OF ENGINEERING CLERMONT-FERRAND
NATIONAL COLLEGE OF ENGINEERING LE MANS

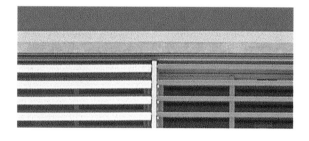

A Different Take on the World

Stan Neumann

To film a building is to enter into a unique relationship with both the object and its architect. It is a very different kind of experience than that of using the building or studying it from a critical point of view – at once lighter, more detached (since I "inhabit" the building only with my eyes and in passing), but nevertheless genuine and intense insofar as I am making a film and as everybody knows there is no film without a love story.

Before filming Christian's buildings, exploring them in this particular fashion, I had already had a first-hand experience of his work simply by living in the 11th arrondissement. I enjoyed walking past the nursery on the rue Saint-Maur, one of the rare success stories in contemporary architecture in this area of Paris. Later, while shooting the film, I became aware of the discontent of local residents along the riverbank who were petitioning against the "brutality" of the building. I could not have been more surprised. Its double curve, gentle and asymmetrical, had always seemed to me particularly at home in the landscape of Parisian neighborhood streets. Jutting out from the line of buildings just enough to announce its presence without threatening the order of the street. An ironic yet respectful interpretation in the great tradition of Haussmann, right down to its emphasis on the facade. And during the shoot, I felt that the concrete of the facade entered into a completely natural dialogue with the hewed stone and the wrought iron of the surrounding buildings.

The first building by Hauvette on which I did any serious work as a filmmaker was the Education Authority of Martinique, devised in a quasi-mythological concept as an office building whose air-conditioning is provided by the region's trade wind. Altogether a powerful experience and not only due to the presence of this particular wind. As we were shooting the film I had the feeling that the building was always changing, in a strange, elusive way. I remember saying to myself: "This is a magnificent building. From any angle, from any perspective, it constantly reveals itself in new images with great generosity. At the same time, you can't grasp precisely its inner space, its ever changing perspectives give you no room to rest, to stay put – you enter by one side and without even realizing it you are already on the other side, outside. So you are constantly on the move just like the air streams passing through."

Here, I encountered for the first time a dream of 20th century architecture come true: a building where no frontier exists between inside and outside, a building without walls, altogether made to be swept by winds and by the human eye. People like to compare this building to a sailboat, but for me it worked more like a viewfinder, a frame, a machine that produces ever new landscapes, new vistas. It's for me the absolute opposite of the fortress-like Polytechnic School of Clermont-Ferrand whose stone walls resolutely turn their back on the idea of transparency in order to work with opacity, material monumentality.

As a filmmaker, I am a priori ill-disposed toward large buildings, which I find much more difficult to film, their dimensions overwhelming to the eye of the camera – a small instrument that is by nature intimate. And yet I do admire monumental architecture. I love how it unsettles me, how it forces me to think on a different level of space and time. I like the massive and deliberate homogeneity of Clermont (in contrast to the abundance of images in the Rectorat) simply because of the story it tells. The way its great elliptical form rejects the "modernity" surrounding it, fighting against the lawless suburban trash with the venerable weapons of symmetry, regularity and scale. As is so often the case with Christian, the story goes against the grain. It is an architectural morality tale that is edifying – as I'm almost tempted to say, without any malice. An affirmation of shared public values against the jungle of market architecture and the banal glorification of the architectural ego.

My first encounter with a building is like a first date with a person. Great expectations mixed with the fear of being disappointed, of feeling no desire, no interest in filming. Something has to click, not necessarily with regard to the architectural quality. If all I had found at ENSIM had been a facade of moveable glass panels, revisiting one of the ideas realized in the Rectorat but more subtly and more stunningly plastic, I would have found it merely beautiful. A variant, nothing to set desire in motion. But inside the building interior there are these great wells of light, three glass cages filled with vegetation, cadencing the length of the main corridor. It's hard to imagine anything more simple or minimal. Yet the positioning of the glass panels, slightly off the right angle, sets something in motion: an invitation to dream. I could have stayed for hours looking at the play of shadows and silhouettes projected through these wells onto the floor. I still don't know whether they have a particular purpose and it didn't enter my mind to ask Christian, though for me they are the embodiment of this building.

Milena Jesenska, Kafka's Milena, said: "To discover a landscape through a window is to discover it doubly, by sight and by desire." I have always had a passion for windows. They are featured in all my films and I undoubtedly chose film making to have an excuse for looking through them. Christian's work has provided ample fuel for this passion and new possible answers to the enigma of the window, the almost metaphysical difficulties posed by the simple act of opening a hole in a wall. The "curse of architecture" as he himself puts it.

Circumventing this malediction seems sometimes the real object of his work. I am thinking, for example, of the metal shutters on the small towers in Rennes. I admire the economy of these two small towers, which give themselves no airs, placed there without arrogance and yet with great awareness of their autonomy. Compared to the surrounding wasteland, these are the only objects with a bit of dignity, with a violent yet integrated esthetic that moves me deeply, with their twinship, two small solitary towers, like the embryo of the real city to come. And then there are those metallic perforated shutters, endlessly recasting the image of the facade. I first discovered them in the evening, from the outside, that archetypal image of windows lit at night, intimate images projected onto the screen of the facade, here filtered through these punctured shutters, more Chinese shadow play than keyhole. Then, on the following morning, as the two towers basked in a pale sun – metal shiny against concrete – we took one last shot from inside one of the apartments. And the plain view of a mean suburban street suddenly became utterly moving as I looked at it through this simple filter, which broke it into small fragments and yet kept it always one.

As often with Christian the image of this puzzle brings back in my memory its utter opposite: the large single window of the south facade of the building in the Impasse Marteau, built on the shore of this sea of cars that is the Paris ring road. This elongated and sealed window ensures perfect sound insulation against the bypass that is only a few meters away. You are inside the apartment and cars glide by in the window, soundlessly at 90 kilometers an hour as if on a screen, or even better, in a kind of inverted aquarium. The ring road seen this close should be one of the ugliest sights ever, but thus silenced and framed, it regains a kind of human grace. That is maybe what Christian means when he speaks of transforming urban wilderness into a place to be.
I have never been obsessed with convergences between different disciplines and I have never believed in some kind of mysterious affinity that would predestine architecture and the cinema for each other. Yet in listening to Christian and filming his buildings, I have often been touched by a different, unexpected affinity between architecture and the cinema that I love. I feel that the purpose of architecture is not only to provide shelter and fulfill functions, but also to change our perception of the world at large.

This building is constructed alongside a railroad track on a lozenge-shaped lot in the context of a "new town."

The program is to accommodate a school of photography and film, with lecture rooms, film studios and laboratories. The structure is composed of two parallel bars set on either side of a covered "passage."

Like a cruise ship at its quay, the complex is lashed to a raised road and parallel to a track by means of heavy concrete walls, which are slightly out of plumb and thus support the two thick "slabs" for photography and film, respectively.

The concrete walls protect the film studios and laboratories. The film that encircles the building is the facade of the class rooms. The crown is reserved for the building installations from which the fluids that are indispensable to the operation of this project are distributed.

Project Team
Architect: Christian Hauvette

Client
Ministry of National Education

Developer
SCARIF

Floor area: 5,400 m^2
Cost: 48 million francs (before tax)
Cost per m^2: 8,888 francs (before tax)/m^2
Completion: September 1988

NATIONAL COLLEGE LOUIS LUMIÈRE

NOISY-LE-GRAND 1986 | 1988

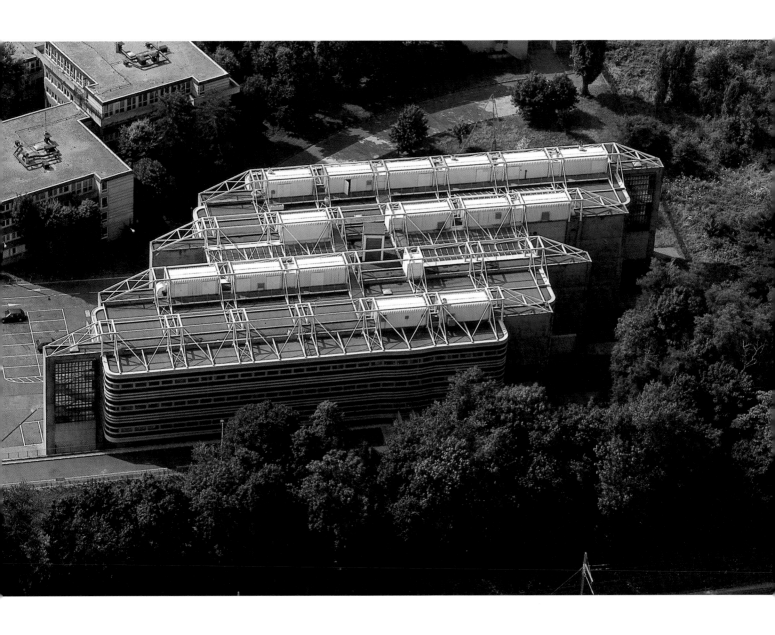

Aerial view taken in October 1999

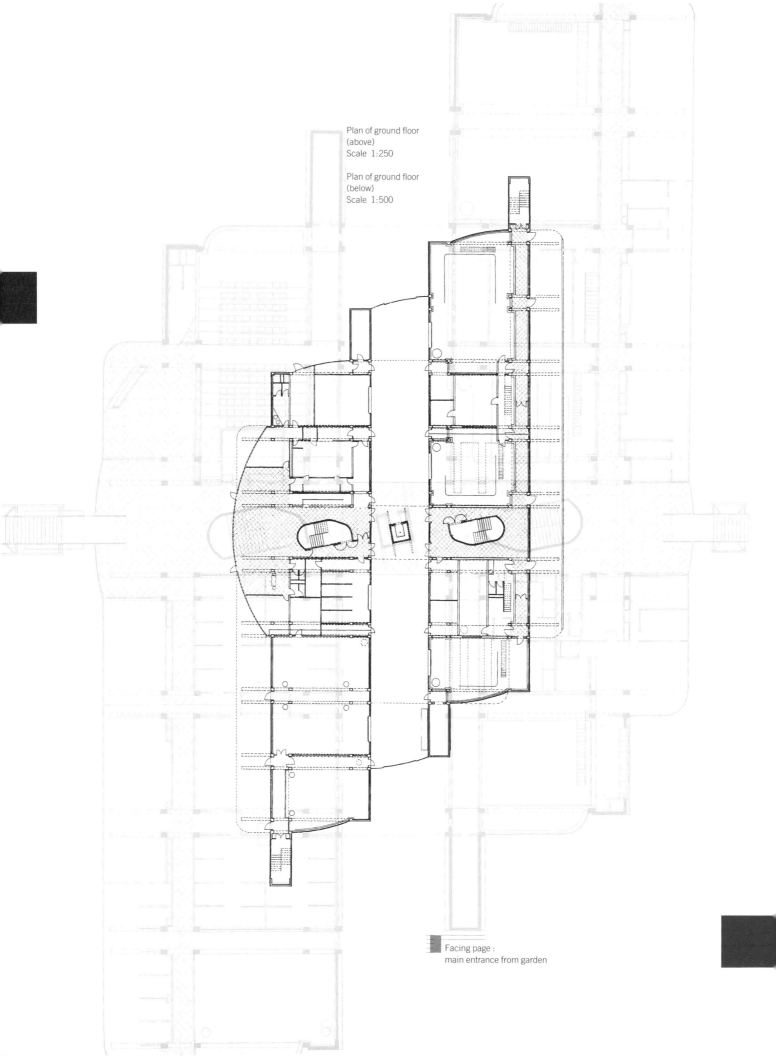

Plan of ground floor
(above)
Scale 1:250

Plan of ground floor
(below)
Scale 1:500

Facing page :
main entrance from garden

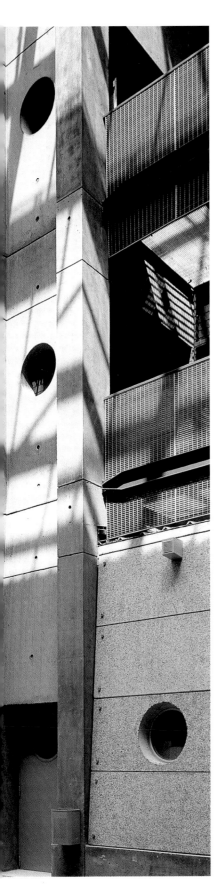

The load-bearing structure in black concrete cast-in-place, onto which the horizontal "planks" in pebbled concrete are bolted

Partitions of the photo building: red
Partitions of the film building: blue

What makes this building – an experiment in construction with regard to climate – so original is that it was conceived to dispense with mechanical air conditioning although that method is often used in the climate of Martinique.

The architecture was carefully designed to accommodate the requirements of working conditions in a humid tropical climate. The idea is to capture the trade wind and to let it gently flow through the building, thus bringing a refreshing breeze into each office. The standard use of walls as fixed screens has been excluded from this project. They are replaced by a mixture of longitudinal porticos in reinforced concrete, cross braced with Saint-André steel crosses.

The rabbets in the fine concrete skeleton provide a precise fit for the mobile infill components (slatted blinds and shutters), the fixed or mobile components of the internal partitions (partitions and louvered doors), and the fixed components for protection (rain protection, sunshades).

Project Team
Architect: Christian Hauvette
Associate architect: Jérôme Nouel

Client
Ministry of Education

Developer
S.C.O.S.U

Floor area: 8,250 m^2
Cost: 73 million francs (before tax)
Cost per m^2: 8,848 francs (before tax)/m^2
Completion: January 1994

EDUCATION AUTHORITY OF MARTINIQUE

FORT-DE-FRANCE 1989 | 1994

Situated on the windy plateau
of Terreville, the building
dominates over the disorder
of the pavilion structures.

The great curved facade overlooks
the bay of Fort-de-France.

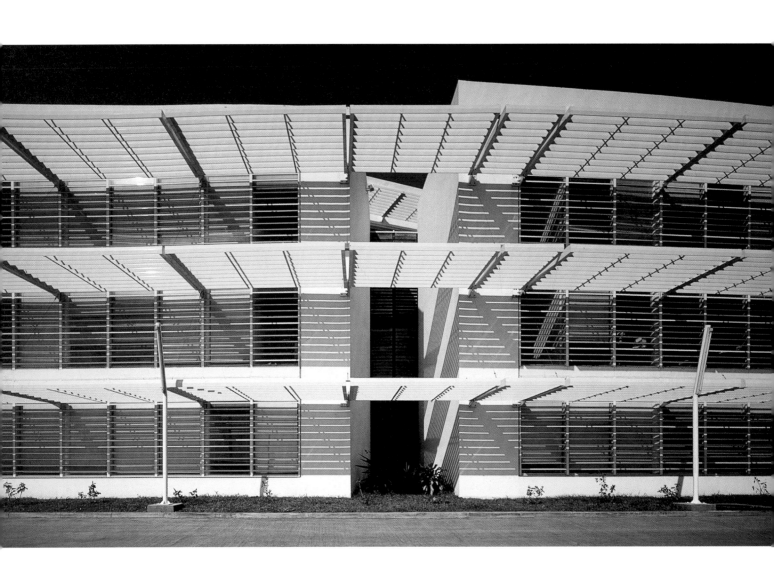

To the south, the convex facade "under the wind" accentuates the low air pressure as a result of its curved shape.

To the north, the straight facade serves
as an "air catch" for the entire building.

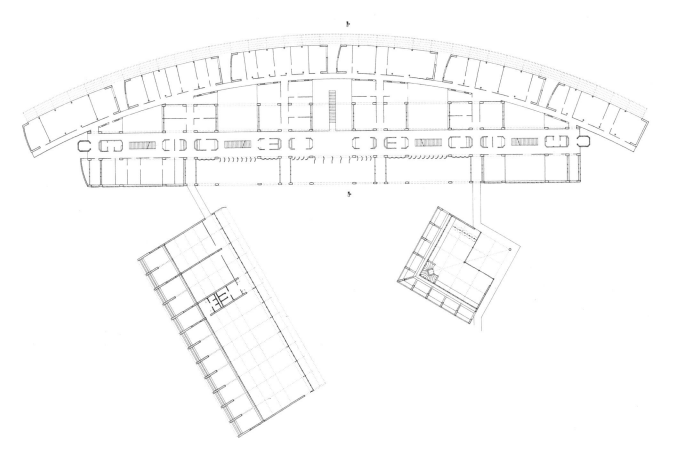

Floor plan of
ground floor, top

Scale 1:750

The structure is a combination of longitudinal porticos in reinforced concrete
cross-braced with Saint-André steel
crosses. This systematic structure
has no windows. The concrete frames
are arranged on parallel east-west lines,
the steel crosses on perpendicular
north-south lines.

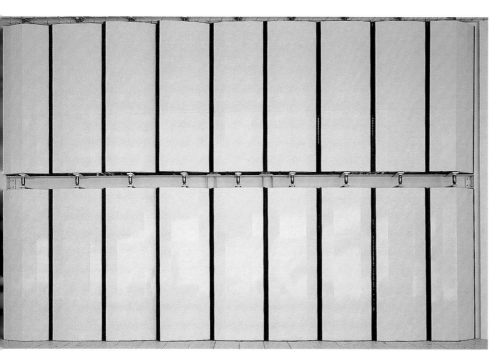

The portico serves as an air catch.
It is equipped with large shutters
on a vertical axis whose opening
mechanism is controlled
by anemometers on the roof.

View above from a patio

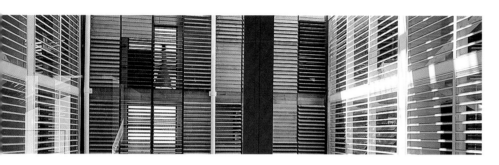

The rabbets in the fine concrete skeleton provide a precise fit for the mobile infill components (slatted blinds and shutters), the fixed or mobile components of the internal partitions (partitions and louvered doors), and the fixed components for protection (rain protection, sunshades).

The modular approach has allowed for on-site installation of finished elements prefabricated in France.

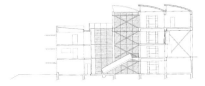

Cross section

Scale 1:750

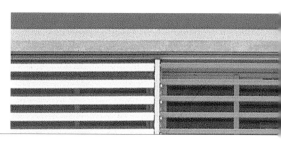

Four simple shapes for four separate functions. Four precious objects set onto the Cézeaux plateau amidst a limitless horizon of mountains.

A square, a diagonal vault and two parallelepipeds accommodate the school, the administration, the research center, and the technology hall. To illustrate the theme of nature "transformed," each building is adorned with shady nooks of vegetation, winter gardens, and rows of trees radically pruned into geometrical shapes. The allusion extends even to the treatment of the infill materials: rough concrete, oxidized wood and steel that is allowed to rust.

One imagines a resident of these surroundings more as a stroller than a poet, his route suffused in green light and his pauses inspired by the quality of his surroundings.

Project Team
Architect: Christian Hauvette
Associate architects: Atelier 4
Landscape architect: David Besson-Girard

Client
CEMAGREF

Developer
SCIC-AMO

Program
Research laboratory and school
of engineering for agricultural engineering
and water and forest management

Floor area: 7,000 m^2
Cost: 51 million francs (before tax)
Cost per m^2: 7,285 francs (before tax)/m^2
Completion: March 1998

RESEARCH CENTER AND SCHOOL OF ENGINEERING

CLERMONT-FERRAND 1994 | 1998

From left to right: technology hall,
research center, administration,
engineering school

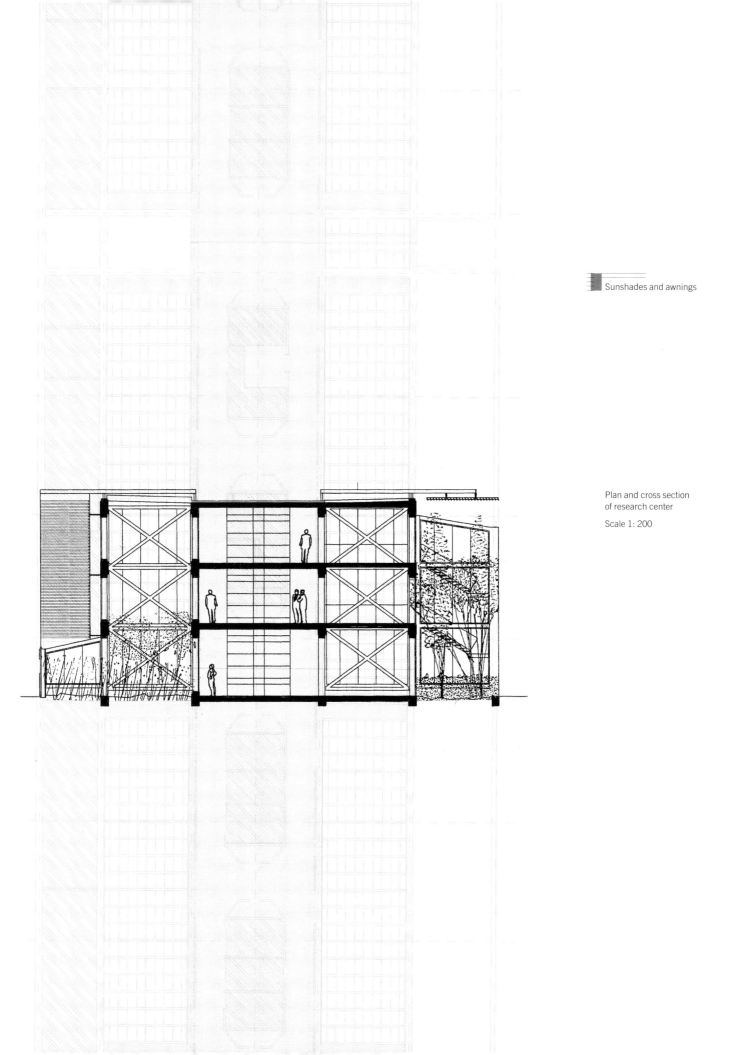

Sunshades and awnings

Plan and cross section
of research center

Scale 1: 200

The structure is a combination of longitudinal porticos in reinforced concrete cross-braced with Saint-André steel crosses.

A wide, longitudinal circulation passage connects the four sections.

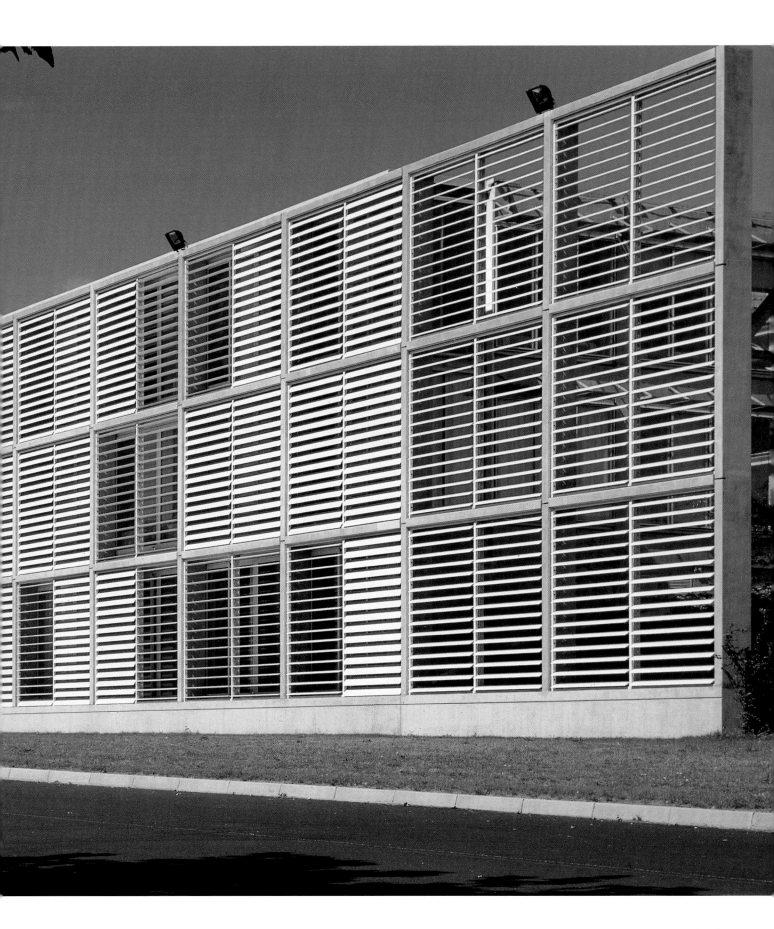

One of those French campuses characterized by vigorous architectural assaults, where urbanity is relegated to the background. Competing against one another, the individual architectures end up canceling each other out. Our task is therefore to construct a "sign zero" building, that distances itself from this formal competition. The site contained a tree-lined sunken path, which we have "folded" and transformed into the spine of our building. It has only one uniform level above the ground floor and has been designed as a very light footprint on this beautiful, inclined terrain, following the set alignments. The internal path provides organization, strewn with irregular copses.

The flat facades also blend into the background for the benefit of natural light, meeting the users' requirements. They are constructed of two successive planes of glass, separated by some sixty centimeters, a buffer that accommodates the structural steel framework, the building services. The external plane is an assemblage of adjustable blinds and glass sheets. The internal plane consists of sliding glass panels.

Project Team
Architect: Christian Hauvette
Associate architect: Bernard Dufournet
Landscape architect: David Besson-Girard

Client
University of Maine

Developer
D.D.E. de la Sarthe

Program
Engineering school and research laboratories

Floor area: 5,000 m^2
Cost: 26,5 million francs (before tax)
Cost per m^2: 5,300 francs (before tax)/m^2
Completion: September 1998

NATIONAL COLLEGE OF ENGINEERING

LE MANS 1995 | 1998

Aerial view of the building in 1999

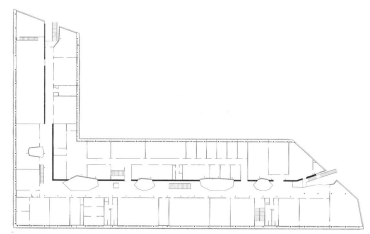

Plan of first floor

Scale 1:1000

Morning aspect of east facade, summer
Morning aspect of east facade, winter

Cross section

Scale 1:250

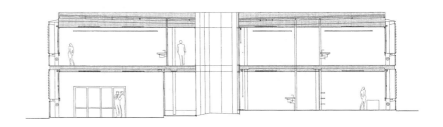

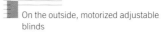 Two planes of glass with a 60 cm space in between. In the interior, simple sliding glass panels

On the outside, motorized adjustable blinds

A series of open-air patios provides light to the interior street whose floor follows the slope of the terrain.

Amphitheater

Laboratory

The slope of the amphitheater
floor matches the incline
in the natural terrain.

Truth, Metaphor, Narrative

Truth

According to one of the few enduring ideas in the history of classic philosophy, truth is a property of verbal propositions, in other words of the formulation, the predicate. "There is no geometry without speech," Socrates says to Phaedra in a conversation on architecture conceived by Paul Valéry. "Without it, shapes are accidents; and neither manifest nor serve the power of the spirit. Through it, the movements that engender the geometric shapes having been reduced to acts that are distinctly denoted by words, each shape is a proposition of potential combination with others; and thus we are able, without further consideration of sight or movement, to recognize the properties of the combinations we have created; constructing or enriching the extension, as it were, by means of well-linked discourse."

Architecture needs language, but it isn't one itself. If a true scientific definition of architecture as language existed, it would make itself known. This proposition is erroneous, however. In fact, to contradict traditional philosophy – which proposes a relationship between the predicate and the object – structural linguistics and semiology have spared no effort in their desire to demonstrate that the word is not the object, and that the articulations of verbal language and of formal language, respectively, are not one and the same. They have summarized these ideas in formulae known as the "arbitrariness of the sign" and "double articulation."

Yet, artists and poets never cease to tell us otherwise. I am thinking in particular of those small poems by Francis Ponge, which have created a unique genre in contemporary literature. Ponge struggles with language to direct it towards an infinite pursuit of things, to transform it into a veritable language of things. The definitive product of his research is undoubtedly represented in the poem *Le Table*, Ponge's final work as a mature poet. Having spent an entire life bent over this object, it becomes, in the end, itself the subject of his scrutiny: the table as ultimate outcome, definitive metaphor of his attitude. Ponge demonstrates that the word table – written as it is with a capital T and its suffix "able," capable – is already contained in the table. The word table *is* the table. The word is contained in the object.

The object is at the root of architecture. Architecture is first and foremost made from objects, before being determined by the space they contain. One might say that architectural space has no meaning on its own, nor yet any property (in the sense of a characteristic). It can be neither expanded, nor contracted, nor orientated; to contradict the notions adopted in the critical jargon. Space is but a void laden with objects that are carriers of evocations and are arranged by force of reason and the coherence of a narrative. It is above all delimited, designated, in some way, before making any claim to being the ultimate stage of architecture.

In the end, the only interest in this idea of comparing architecture to a language lies in pursuing an attitude with regard to the idea of truth, an attitude that involves a steadfast will to achieve it, both in the definition of the objects themselves and in the operation of the rules that determine their configuration.

In an attempt to draw upon these ideas, I would like to reduce the architectural project to two simple terms: object and event. With this hypothesis I propose to consider architectural components as devoid of qualities, that is to say, unaffected by significations, and to look upon them as neutral objects in whose space only identified events that affect the subject take place.

"Object, basic reality, envisioned in a static state and, as it were, separated or separable from the whole world, composed by means of a set system of qualities or properties," reads Lalande's definition in his dictionary of philosophy.

The first quality of this architectural "object" would be its constructibility. Thus I strive to consider architecture exclusively from that which, fundamentally, constitutes it: its material aspect, quantifiable and constructible. Its solidity, as it were. I dream of certainty, that state of mind (experienced) vis-à-vis a judgement one knows to be true, without a shadow of doubt.

"Event, that which befalls or happens to the subject, inasmuch as one considers it to be an experiential given."

One can doubtless propose that in architecture an event is unfailingly linked to an object. In fact, the subject is always faced with this dual reality: it crosses a threshold, it bumps into a wall and hurts itself badly, it falls out of the window and dies, etc. … A staircase, for example, is one of the objects most closely linked to an event, ascending or descending. It is one of the most "denotative" architectural signifiers, the least ambiguous, and one of the most usable in this very simplifying game of an, albeit complex, reality.

Thus I question the possibility of founding a kind of elementary grammar of architecture on the single combination between these notions of object and event, working the idea in a kind of architectural choreography based on that which is certain in the relationships between events and décor, between subject and object. Is it possible to conceive a series of fundamental relationships of this kind without stooping to catalogistic sterility? Will such a framework hold? Is there a theoretical montage of this kind in another discipline?

In any case, this demonstrates my attraction to analytical philosophies, which give me a sense of coming closest to metaphysics without, paradoxically, ever trying to evoke it. In other words, what fascinates me in Ludwig Wittgenstein or in Nelson Goodman, is their ability to string logical progressions together from extremely simple premises, progressions which rapidly reach a vertiginous height that is beyond the reach of reason.

To nourish this ambition, I propose the following definitions and rules of the game:

Architecture: an ensemble of objects in which events take place.

Planning: to arrange built objects with the goal of welcoming events.

Architect: he or she who formalizes architectural demonstrations based on only those premises recognized as true, and proving their truth in construction.

Metaphor

Geometry: one of the simplest grammatical systems used to govern how objects are arranged in a space, a geometry that has more in common with the poet's propositions than with a land surveyor's. Metric rather geometric, I would have to say.

One knows to which degree, during the creation of a work, language games can be rendered sterile unless they are accompanied and enriched by the appropriate evocations. The value of a poetic work, for example, lies in the correct apportionment of versification, images and narrative.

And so I turn my attention to a second plane: the plane of the imagination. Since I know little about the theories of imagination, I take the liberty of examining it from two angles which seem (self-)evident to me and which I shall call: inborn imagination, on the one hand, and transferred or assembled imagination on the other.

Is there a brute imagination, an imagination that draws its nourishment from common locales, which habitually crowds the human brain to appear in all its splendour? The general view seems to define native imagination as a capacity for invention, a kind of innate ability that is the exclusive domain of the chosen few, singled out by their superhuman powers. I admit to having had similar experiences while teaching: the quasi-miraculous apparition of a surprising form that contains and summarizes functions for which it was not conceived. Unfortunately, that is all I am able to say on the subject and so I move on, instead, to look at metaphor from the second aspect of imagination.

Much has been said in rhetoric, ancient and new, about the nature of metaphors. I appreciate the clarity of Nelson Goodman's propositions on the subject, the idea of "calculated categorical transfers," of which above all, the foremost expression – calculated – is important to me as an architect. Calculation calls to mind the issue of controlling metaphors within the work on the project, the "projetation" as design is called in my native tongue. The difficulties lie in taming them rather than in their nature. There are many dangers in the use of metaphors, one being the trend to inexorably link them to the common locale where they are taken as a kind of incontestable fact, as the naturalness of the sign. In fact, these images become all the more literal as their newness fades; in our mediated world these painful allegories wear off all too easily. Even worse, they occupy a site and install themselves in lieu of reality, manifesting a reality inverted by the vigorously denounced spectacle.

As is the case in many other artistic disciplines, imagination in architecture consists in putting the image – that is the evocative force – into the project. The topic of the mediating role of the borrowed image – the metaphor – in the relationship between form and meaning has been exhaustively explored. There's nothing left to say. The image is everywhere. Beyond the materiality, which I criticized above, I believe that it is possible to affirm a total absence of denotation of the architectural sign, even usage would not constitute an irreducible core of meaning, its ultimate reality. Any architectural sign is at the very least double: it does not want to be what it is, it wants to be the other. Architecture consists entirely of these real objects with simulated doubles. Therein lies the paradox.

Thus, for the first time, I am trying to invoke a kind of halo of images from which I choose and convoke those that are necessary to my practice. Needless to specify that I dismiss without hesitation any that do not fulfill the functions for which they were envisioned. The images are drawn from two distinct sources: the first, intrinsic to the discipline, consists in my architectural knowledge and in that of my agency, and the other, extrinsic, consists in familiar cultural spheres that interest me: literature, music, mechanics, technology, for example.

"Unexpected transfer of calculated categorical errors," as Goodman puts it so well, these images, with all their mechanisms of organization, take possession of new territories designated for them. We have all noticed the rejuvenating and fortuitous convergences over which they preside. We don't give a damn about the dangers to which they may lead.

However, there are several problems in this tale of metaphors. One is the danger of going overboard. I'm always wary of objectivizing this imagination, be it for fear of no longer being able to control the unforeseen eruption, or for fear of letting myself be carried away by a particular charm that, in hindsight, reveals itself as worthless. I work at mastering these forces which, when left to the unconscious, might inflict I know not which ravages on the project. Clearly, projects that are founded only on metaphors produce the disastrous effect of pseudo-poetry and usually go hand in hand with mercantile gestures. The cynical attitude this induces in the creator when he exploits its material value first and foremost in order to convince, must be superseded to the benefit of a spirit that considers it as an efficient medium, albeit for temporary or strictly private use.

Thus my work splits into two parallel tracks, one for the creative process – where images are summoned and dismissed in order to put them into forms – and the other for reasoning – where each piece is defined and articulated as if in a great societal game. Two autonomous tracks of parallel operation in a great machine whose engine is the third term. An engine that I shall call: Narrative.

Narrative

"Narratives" serve to refine the elaboration of a project and give a definitive coherence and meaning to the architectural object. During the planning phase, these narratives about the project turn into veritable fairy tales pouring from the architect's lips, part magical invocation, part supplication in an effort to bend reality. One of their functions is to sift through the principal components of the project, bringing them into the open for examination and evaluation in order to modify and reassemble them into new narratives, histories that shed light on new objects, etc. The narratives engender version after version, in a rapid forward movement, in the knowledge that each is ever so slightly different from the previous, presenting unforeseen progressions. They facilitate a view of the project from the perspective of sober evaluation and simultaneously give permission to the observer to fall under the spell of a particularly charming story. Propelled forward by these narratives, the project unfolds bit by bit until it finds itself, at best, in the grip of some miracle of signification, a miracle that is effective only if it also makes sense to the commissioning client.

This is where it gets interesting. Namely, when narratives that give meaning to the work – general narratives with some relation to the questions posed, or more private ones presented by the author himself– circulate within and outside of the project, hold it together, guarantee coherence and pertinence, make it playful somehow, not only in the eyes of the author, but also in those of the user.

This explains why the metaphor of *The Castle of Crossed Destinies*, a novelette by Italo Calvino, is one of my favourite metaphors for architecture. One night, pilgrims traverse a dense forest and come upon a castle. They enter but soon discover that they have been rendered mute. The master of the house invites them to a table and puts a tarot game at their disposal. Each tells his personal history through the cards he selects and through completing the game of the others. Each guest silently constructs his own interpretation. Finally, the spell is broken: when they regain speech, the pilgrims discover that they have all fabricated different versions. But all admire the work spread out before them on the table.

I like to look upon the project of architecture as a great card game in which the laws of assemblage, metaphors, the combination of shapes, narratives and interpretations are put into balance. In this game, the final configuration weighs more than the sum of its components.

The true work abolishes the rules that created it. It destroys the metaphors. It forgets the narratives. It functions without parasites.

I propose to call such an architectural object: Machine. A word that should not be taken in the functional and pedagogic sense developed by the architects of the modern movement, but in its literary sense. In the sense used by Roland Barthes, for example, when he strives to shed light on the relationship between imagination and mechanics, insisting on creating laws of specific organization, unveiled as such and systematically explored, an image, precisely, which Italo Calvino calls the "literary machine."

Generating machine: cogs, structures, facades, occupancy, floors, partitions, etc., exist simultaneously as autonomous objects and as extrinsic meanings, because they entail, because they produce: evocations, meaning. Physical cogs that produce virtual cogs in one and the same movement. If my premise focuses primarily on the former, it is to subsequently better succeed with the latter.

When, as I have explained, I methodologically dissociate the appeal of ideas, mechanisms and narratives, this is not with the intention of losing sight of the globality of architecture. By making use of distinct yet fusional ingredients, I proceed in the manner of the chef, the composer and the poet. Each element must, at the very least, be identifiable and yet participate in the whole. But this is not enough: when I refine a flat, non-perspective vision of my projects during the production phase, I do so in order to make each a construction that is true in spirit rather than a mere physical covering. I try to substitute the idea of reading for the notion of spatial perception. To propose the right object in which all the theory and metaphors that created it in the first place recede into the background. To my viewer, my reader, I offer a cold machine based on a system of plain values, far from metaphysical evocation since its production rests solely on a strict appreciation of the reality of things.

The "architectural machine" is not intended to fuse with the construct that hems it in. It is not intended for integration. The machine should be perceived, contemplated. With the exception of a few very specific locales, some ancient centers, urban space can today be regarded as a kind of breeding-ground for indifference composed of a multitude of objects, which neutralize one another. My problem with this definition is to produce projects of great internal coherence, whose concepts embody a structure which society no longer wishes to give to the space that surrounds them. Space is no place, a void. Space interests me only as the result of a work on objects. What fascinates me in material objects is as much their presence, their form, their capacity to enunciate as their manner of organization, combination and configuration into language games. We must coax them out of their hiding place, bring them out into the light of day. This, I suppose, goes beyond a simple narcissistic investment of the architect himself, or his culture, or his talent, into the work.

The latter is merely a visual instrument intended to show us the framework. One should note, here, the unanimity of this discourse on the valuation of the framework, as the authorities are always in need of stage designers. Conversely, the architectural object is a complete instrument, autonomous, which does not add to the disorder but feeds off of it. I install it on its site in a manner that is not in the least mimetic, but instead polemic. This object which I project illuminates nothing, suggests no specific reading of that which surrounds it. On the contrary, it is the environment that dissolves into it. I use the site to bring it to light, to coax it from the ground. The framework sheds light on the object.

But after all, this tale of the object nourished by context is but a hypothesis. Perhaps, the mechanism could also operate in reverse and the object would, in turn, obscure the context, neutralize it, pacify it, and contaminate it. The price I pay for tying in with the locale, the agreement, a gesture of politeness, is returned to my advantage if I've done my work well. Eventually, the object can link up with the site to reach its conclusion, doubtless the only way to become a true work, the least autonomous, the most indexed to a network of "correspondences," the most situated, as Charles Baudelaire suggested.

Christian Hauvette

Christian Hauvette
7 rue Debelleyme
75003 Paris

1969   Certified architect

1969   Diploma in Urbanism
       from the Institut d'Urbanisme
       de l'Université de Paris

Major awards

1999   Medal of Honor,
       Academy of Architecture

1997   Knight of Arts and Letters

1994   Tenured Professorship,
       Schools of Architecture

1993   Knight of the Ordre National
       du Mérite

1991   National Award
       for Architecture

1989   Knight of the Order
       of Palmes Académiques
       (services to education)
       Silver Medal (Prix Dejean)
       of the Academy of Architecture

1986   First Prize, Public Buildings
       (Interdepartmental
       brief for Quality
       in Public Buildings)

Projects

**Office building in Paris,
13th arrondissement (1998)**
Savings and Loans Bank
Competition, award-winning project
in progress

71 Housing units, Rennes (1996)
ARC Promotion
Commission, completed in 1999

**National College of Engineering,
Le Mans (1995)**
University of Maine
Competition, award-winning project,
completed in 1999

**Branch office for French Development
Agency, Paris, 12th arrondissement (1994)**
Agence Française de Développement
Competition, award-winning project,
completed in 1998

**CEMAGREF-ENGREF at Clermont-Ferrand
(1994)**
CEMAGREF
Competition, award-winning project,
completed in 1998

166 Housing units, Rennes (1992)
OCODIM
Commission, completed in 1997

**82 Social housing units, Paris, 18th
arrondissement (1991)**
OPAC de Paris
Commission, completed in 1996

**204 Housing units for police officers,
Paris, 18th arrondissement (1990)**
Ministry of the Interior (DEPAFI)
Competition, award-winning project,
completed in 1994

Major competitions since 1990

Education Authority of Martinique,
Fort-de-France (1989)
Ministry of Education (SCOSU)
Competition, award-winning project,
completed in 1994

Lafayette Polytechnic School,
Clermont-Ferrand (1988)
Auvergne Region
Competition, award-winning project,
completed in 1991

Primary school and nursery for 10
classes, Montigny-le-Bretonneux (1987)
SAN of Saint-Quentin en Yvelines
Competition, award-winning project,
completed in 1989

National College Louis Lumière, Noisy-
le-Grand (1986)
Ministry of Education, SCARIF
Competition, award-winning project,
completed in 1989

Nursery for 80 children, Paris,
11th arrondissement (1986)
City of Paris
Commission, completed in 1990

Regional audit house of Brittanny,
Rennes (1985)
Ministry of Finance
Competition, award-winning project,
completed in 1988

Faculty of Law and Economics
and Amphitheater, Brest (1984)
Ministry of Education
Competition, award-winning project,
completed in 1986

Offices for the w.o.i.p. in Geneva (2000)
World Organisation for the Protection
of Intellectual Property
Competition by invitation, in progress

Northern regional service center (2000)
Northern Regional Authorities
Competition by invitation, in progress

Theater in Lorient (1999)
Competition by invitation, not awarded

Hospital in Lyon (1999)
Civilian Hospice of Lyon
Competition by invitation, not awarded

Office building for the Savings
and Loans Bank, Paris,
13th arrondissement (1998)
Deposit and Consignment Office
Competition by invitation,
award-winning project

Swimming pool in Le Mans (1998)
City of Le Mans
Competition by invitation, not awarded

Union house in Nantes (1997)
City of Nantes
Competition by invitation, not awarded

Headquarters for Lafarge Plâtres at
Avignon (1996)
Lafarge Plâtres
Competition by invitation, not awarded

Archives of the Fifth Republic at Reims
(1996)
Ministry of Culture, Ministry of Defence
Competition by invitation, not awarded

Courthouse at Fort-de-France (1995)
Ministry of Justice
Competition by invitation, not awarded

School of engineering at Le Mans (1996)
University of Maine. Competition by
invitation, award-winning project

Research center at Clermont-Ferrand
(1994)
CEMAGREF-ENGREF
Competition by invitation,
award-winning project

Headquarters for the French
Development Agency, Paris (1994)
French Development Agency
Competition by invitation,
award-winning project

Courthouse at Nantes (1993)
Ministry of Justice
Competition by invitation, not awarded

National school of Mining Engineering
at Nantes (1992)
Public Administration of the National
School of Technology,
Industry and Mining at Nantes
Competition by invitation,
project selected for second round

Urban development of Lower Montreuil
(1991)
City of Montreuil
Competition by invitation,
award-winning project

Post-graduate school in Law
and Economics at Amiens (1991)
Regional Council of Picardy
Competition by invitation,
project selected for second round

French Pavilion at the World Exhibition
in Seville (1980)
COFRES (French Organisation
for the World Exhibition in Seville)
Competition, project selected for
second round

Publications

1997 *Christian Hauvette*
Current Architecture Catalogues /
Monografías de arquitectura
Editions Gustavo Gili, Barcelona

1996 *Crosscurrents*
Fifty-one world Architects –
Christian Hauvette
Editor SYNECTICS INC. Tokyo

1995 *La boîte à vent*
Education Authority
for the Academy of the Antilles
and Guyana
Editions Sens & Tonka, Paris

1994 *Christian Hauvette*
Collection Gros-Plans
Institut Français d'Architecture,
Paris

1993 *Arquitectura francesa, 11 proyectos*
Architecture Studio, Hauvette,
Nouvel, Perrault
Editions Junta de Andalucia,
Seville

1991 *Suite… sans fin*
Editions Pandora, Paris

1989 *The New French Architecture*
Editions Rizzoli, New York

1989 *Croiseur Lumière*
Editions du Demi-Cercle, Paris

1988 *La Chambre*
Editions du Demi-Cercle, Paris

1987 *Hauvette, Hondelatte, Soler*
Editions Arc-en-Rêve, Bordeaux

Teaching and research

1998 Visiting professor at the Virginia
Polytechnic Institute, College
of Architecture (Virginia, USA)

1994 Tenured professor at the School
of Architecture, Brittany

1993 Visiting professor at the
University of Houston
(Texas, USA)

1992– Member of the Council
1993 for Science and Teaching
in Architecture

1991 Visiting professor
at the School of Architecture
at Clermont-Ferrand

1990 Visiting professor at the Virginia
Polytechnic Institute, College
of Architecture (Virginia, USA)

1974– In charge of teaching at the
1975 University de Paris VII,
Postgraduate "Social Sciences"

1974 Grant holder, Group for Research
and Experimentation
in Cinematography (GREC)

1972– Postgraduate student at the
1974 Applied School of Higher Studies.
Thesis supervisor:
Roland Barthes

1965– Student at the National School
1967 of Engineering and Technology,
studies under Jean Prouvé

Exhibitions

1999 École Polytechnique Fédérale
de Lausanne, Switzerland
"Variations," Christian Hauvette –
Architect

1998 Tajima Gallery, Tokyo, Japan
"Partitions," Christian Hauvette –
Architect
Exhibition as part of the
'Year of France' in Japan

1997 GA Gallery, Tokyo, Japan
"Six French Architects"
Architecture Studio, F. Boret,
C. Hauvette, M. Kagan,
D. Perrault, F. Soler

1993 Seville, Spain
"Arquitectura francesa,
11 proyectos"
Architecture Studio, Hauvette,
Nouvel, Perrault

1993 Institut d'Art Visual, Orléans,
France
"Hauvette, architecte"

1991 Institut Français d'Architecture,
Paris, France
"Christian Hauvette,
Suite… sans fin… 36 projets"

1990 Chicago Graham Foundation,
USA
"Paris meets Chicago,
9 leading french architects"

1990 Institut Français d'Architecture,
Paris, France
"Pavillon de la France à Séville"

1990 Centre Georges Pompidou, Paris,
France
"Architectures Publiques"

Articles and Interviews

1989	The Art Institute of Chicago, USA "French Avant Garde"	
1988	École d'Architecture, Clermont-Ferrand, France "Hauvette: cinq bâtiments publics"	
1988	Galerie Arc-en-Rêve, Bordeaux, France "Hauvette-Hondelatte-Soler"	
1988	Institut Français d'Architecture, Paris, France "Grands Projets Culturels en France"	
1988	New York, USA "Grands Projets Parisiens"	
1988	Palais de Chaillot, Paris, France Interdepartmental exhibition on quality in public buildings "Architectures Publiques"	

Christian Hauvette
Interview, *In-Ex revue périphérique d'architecture*,
Birkhäuser – Publishers for Architecture,
Basel, Boston, Berlin – October 1999

Patrimoine et Citoyenneté
Contribution, Ministry of Culture and Communication/
France Loisirs, Paris – September 1999

Hauvette chez T.G.T.
Contribution, Le bulletin d'informations
architecturales, IFA, Paris – April 1999

Francis Soler
Contribution, Archimade No. 65, Geneva –
December 1997

Francis Soler, architect
Introduction, "Gros-Plan" (Close-up), IFA, Paris –
June 1994

Nemo
Preface, "mnémo, architecture de mémoire"
Editions Caisse des Dépots, Paris – January 1994

Christian Hauvette
Interview, Les architectes et la construction,
Editions Technique et Architecture, Paris – January 1994

Construire à Paris
Contribution, Archimade No. 42, Geneva –
December 1993

Christian Hauvette
Interview, Cahiers de la Recherche Architecturale No. 31,
"Concevoir," Paris – 4th quarter 1993

Toyo Ito: the Path between Abstraction and Metaphor,
Contribution, The Japan Architect Library, Tokyo –
Summer 1993

Un coffre à bébés
Contribution, Archimade No. 40, Geneva – June 1993

Architecture et Art
Contribution, Architecture d'Aujourd'hui No. 286, Paris
– April 1993

Fonde l'amour des tours
Contribution, Alliage, quarterly, Paris – Spring 1993

Débat, Henri Ciriani
Contribution, Architecture d'Aujourd'hui No. 282, Paris
– September 1992

Dessinez, enfants!
Contribution, Ville d'enfants/Children's village, Groupe
SCIC, l'idée juste, Paris – April 1992

La qualité architecturale
Contribution, Du territoire au project, symposium
proceedings, Paris – November 1991

Philippe Deslandes
Contribution, Deslandes par Deslandes, Regards,
Tempera Editions, Paris – September 1989

La Crèche
Contribution, Architecture et compagnie No.1,
Editions du Demi-cercle, Paris – October 1988

Tonka l'Utopiste
Contribution, Ecrire, dessiner un livre d'architecture,
Centre Pompidou, Paris – February 1988

Le dessin d'architecture
Contribution, Pignon sur rue No. 67, Lyon –
3rd quarter, 1986

Denis Pondruel, sculpteur Français
Contribution, Exhibition catalogue, Galerie Riedel,
Paris – February 1985

Le pain noir
Contribution, H. revue de l'habitat social No. 81,
Paris – January 1983

Décembre au bord de la mer
Contribution, Aller-simple No. 3, quarterly,
Paris – February 1982

Furieux paradigmes et contradictions révélées
Contribution, with Michel Gravayal, Jean Nouvel,
Martin Robain
Architecture, Mouvement, Continuité, Paris –
November 1981

Hommage à Roland Barthes
Contribution, Journal du Syndicat de l'Architecture,
Paris – September 1980

Face à la feuille blanche
Contribution, Journal du Syndicat de l'Architecture,
Paris – February 1980

Doctrines, certitudes
Contribution, Cahiers de la Recherche Architectural
No. 6-7, Paris – October 1980

This book has been realized with
the support of:
. Caisse des Dépôts et Consignations
  (Savings and Loans Bank),
. SEMAPA – Société d'Aménagement Parisienne
  (Urban Development Society, Paris),
. Société de Rénovation Rennaise
  (The Renovation and Restauration Society
  of Rennes),
. EDF (the French Electricity Board),
. the Lafarge group,
. the SCIC group,
. the Goyer Bel company,
. the Erco Lumières company,
. the SB Ballestrero company.

The publishers wish to thank all those
who participated and assisted in
the realization of this publication:
Paul Ardenne, Nicolas Borel,
Kurt Brunner, Georges Fessy,
Christian Hauvette, Véronique Jesse,
Alice Laguarda, Didier Laroque,
Marie Menant, Stan Neumann,
Elisabeth Pistorio, Denis Pondruel,
Luciana Ravanel, Elizabeth Schwaiger,
Barry Stanton, Robert Steiger.

This book is also available in a French
language edition at Jean-Michel Place,
Paris, ISBN 2-85893-541-6.

Translation from French into English:
Elizabeth Schwaiger, Toronto

Proofreader:
Barry Stanton, Lausanne

Illustration Credits:
© Archipress:
page 154.
© Nicolas Borel:
pages 4 (middle), 8, 9, 11, 13, 21, 22,
23 (left), 28, 29, 31, 33, 34-35, 36-37,
39, 41, 42-43, 44, 45, 46-47,
56 (bottom), 59, 63, 64-65 (bottom),
73, 75, 101, 102-103, 104, 116, 127,
128, 129 (bottom), 131, 132, 133,
137, 138-139, 140-141, 142, 143,
144, 145, 146, 147.
© Christophe Demonfaucon:
pages 56 (top), 57.
© Georges Fessy:
pages 4 (bottom), 7, 12, 14, 74, 76, 77,
80, 82, 83, 84, 85, 105, 107, 108, 109,
111, 112, 113, 114, 115, 117, 118, 119,
120, 121, 122, 123, 124-125.
© Khalfi:
page 81.
© Jean-Marie Monthiers:
page 79.
© Marcus Robinson:
pages 4 (top), 15, 23 (right), 24, 25, 26-
27, 30, 54, 55, 58, 60, 61, 64-65 (top),
66, 67, 68, 69, 70, 71.
© Olivier Wogensky:
pages 10, 129 (top), 134-135.

A CIP catalogue record for this book
is available from the Library of Congress,
Washington D.C., USA.

Deutsche Bibliothek Cataloging-in-
Publication Data

Christian Hauvette:
dwellings - monuments - machines ;
truth - metaphor - narrative / with a pref.
by Alice Laguarda and Paul Ardenne
and with texts by Christian Hauvette …
[Transl. from French into Engl.:
Elizabeth Schwaiger]. - Basel ; Boston ;
Berlin : Birkhäuser, 2000
ISBN 3-7643-6233-2

© 2000 Birkhäuser – Publishers
for Architecture, P.O. Box 133,
CH-4010 Basel, Switzerland.
www.birkhauser.ch
© 2000 Éditions Jean-Michel Place,
3 rue Lhomond, F-75005 Paris, France.
www.jmplace.com
© 2000 Christian Hauvette,
7 rue Debelleyme, F-75003 Paris, France.

Printed on acid-free paper produced
from chlorine-free pulp. TCF ∞

Production and coordination:
Ante Prima Consultants

Graphic Design:
martin.brunner.associés, Paris

Printed in France

ISBN 3-7643-6233-2

9 8 7 6 5 4 3 2 1